DISCOVERING
purpose
FOR YOUR LIFE

TODD AARON

Ocean Wave
Ministries ®

This is a work of creative nonfiction.
Copyright © Todd Aaron, 2025
Copyright © 2025 Todd Aaron
Copyright © 2025 by Todd Aaron
All rights reserved. No part of this book may be reproduced in any form or by any electronic or mechanical means, including information storage and retrieval systems, without written permission from the publisher, except for a reviewer who may quote brief passages in a review.

First edition: March 2025
This edition first published in 2025
Illustrations copyright © 2025 by Todd Aaron
Cover photography copyright © Todd Aaron 2025
Cover images/Canva
Design by Todd Aaron
Edited by: Braelyn Locey

All Bible verses in this book are taken from the American Standard Version (ASV) of the Bible (1901), which is in the public domain.

ISBN: 979-8-218-63452-0 (paperback and ebook)
Published by Todd Aaron & Ocean Wave Ministries
www.oceanwaveministries.com
oceanwaveministries@gmail.com

There is a life waiting to be discovered, yet very few will ever find their purpose on a path that no one else can travel. The journey will only be found when you are ready to create new tracks and leave old footprints in the past. Laying down your old life and living out a brand-new life of purpose!

Book Contents

CHAPTER 1: QUESTION YOUR PURPOSE 1

CHAPTER 2: PURPOSE WITH PEACE 6

CHAPTER 3: MY PURPOSE SOUGHT PURPOSE LOST 12

CHAPTER 4: MOTIVATIONS OF PURPOSE 19

CHAPTER 5: DISCOVERING PURPOSE 24

CHAPTER 6: PURPOSE BEYOND LIFE 31

CHAPTER 7: FREEDOM WITH PURPOSE 38

CHAPTER 8: A NEW LIFE 45

CHAPTER 9: WHAT HAS ONE MISSED? 51

CHAPTER 10: DISCOVERING GREATER PURPOSE 57

CHAPTER 11: WHAT IS MY PURPOSE? 63

CHAPTER 12: REMAINING IN PURPOSE WITH PEACE 69

Chapter 1: Question Your Purpose

Every human living throughout life will ponder life's purpose and mysteries. Many will ask, what is my purpose? What is my destiny? Why was I born? Many have already established and discovered their goals and dreams. Some may reach and accomplish those plans, while others are yet to obtain them or may give up altogether. Whether those objectives are achieved or left unfulfilled, both outcomes can still carry a profound longing and purpose buried deep within the soul—an ache so intense that not even the vastest oceans could ever quench it.

One may become successful, wealthy, famous, start a business, or have a humble low-income job and life. Some may get married, have kids, buy a house, buy a few cars, and continue working and climbing the career ladder with raises and promotions. Some might see these achievements as success and a distant goal for others. However, for many, it's their purpose-driven life.

What motivates us to go further, press harder, and even tirelessly with sleepless nights, urges us to go further to achieve life's purpose? What motivates us to get up each day while others choose to end their lives? What motivates people to travel the world while others rarely leave their city, state, community, or country of origin? What motivates some to do whatever it takes to achieve their goals and dreams, while others give up on them and settle with a mediocre life?

Many may find purpose in religion, church, God, or spirituality, while others find it empty and a waste of time. Some people want to live in a city, while others want to live off-grid in the country. Some want to be doctors, while others want to be chefs. Certain people want pets, while others do not want a pet at all. Few may desire to own a mansion, while others want a tiny house or a small van. Some souls desire to play professional sports, while others could care less about sports. Another portion of people love playing instruments and performing music, while others listen. Some want to be leaders, and some want to be followers. Some want to be rich, and others would rather be poor. Some get married or have kids, accomplish marriage, and raise kids until death does them part, while others don't achieve either. Some people do drugs, smoke, or drink alcohol, while others refuse to partake in any of those mind-altering substances. Some see a bright future for themselves, while others see a dim and bleak future. The question is, what motivates people in life and why? Do people take the time to question the motives and driving factors that lead some individuals to keep the gas pedal pressed to the floor while their tank is full, while others let their tank run empty and remain unused?

I once toured the Corvette factory, where my mother, a well-renowned beauty pageant winner, was permitted to start one of the cars, rev the engine in the factory, and was even privileged to keep a copy of its title. It was fascinating that whoever started the engine, whether in the factory or fresh off the lot, acted like someone driving and influencing the vehicle. When you're born, you're like a brand-new car. Who started your engine? Who pressed your gas pedal? Who owns the title of your life? I'm asking, what motivated you from birth to pursue your goals and dreams? What drives your ambition to achieve your aspirations? Are they truly yours?

Some people become influenced by music, TV, parents, friends, communities, coworkers, past boyfriends or girlfriends, social media, YouTube, TikTok, religious leaders, politicians, culture, and other influences shaping and designing one's life. I remember a man from Pakistan who attended school with me in my early years. He could play Beethoven's "Für Elise" better than anyone I've ever heard. His dedication and drive were remarkable; if he missed even one note, he would be incredibly hard on himself, believing he was the worst musician ever. I complimented him on his talent and asked why he was so critical of himself. He replied, "My dad pushes me really hard. When I missed a note, he would smack my hand with a ruler. If I don't perform perfectly, he gives me the silent treatment." This parenting was extreme, I thought. Abuse and neglect were his driving factors, and he had a deep desire to receive his father's praise and approval. He may not have recognized this driving factor, but I did and felt compassion for him.

I've asked doctors in various fields why they chose their occupations. Many said their parents were doctors or encouraged them to become doctors. One urologist out of those many doctors said she chose her specialty because it was her passion. She expressed that she suffered from pain, and one of her family members also suffered severe pain. She hoped to resolve the pain for those close to whom she knew. We see two vastly different motivating factors that drove them to pursue their goals in their life.

I remembered talking with two specific business owners. I asked them, "What brought you to take this path in life?" One was a financial business owner who said, "Money and financial independence." The other was a multiple chain restaurant owner who responded, "Freedom and to give people healthy food options." Which one is a better motivation to pursue? In Jewish culture, striving to become a doctor, lawyer, or having a career in finance is pushed in their families. But what is the motivating factor? Who told them to pursue that goal and why?

We are often taught to start a business if it means benefiting others. I noticed how women-owned or new-age businesses create healthy, holistic, natural, organic beauty, skincare, and food products. On the other hand, conventional companies and corporations focus on money and profits. Women-owned and new-age businesses are putting the health and well-being of others first. I met a woman who owned a dedicated gluten-free restaurant and bakery for those with Celiac Disease. After thanking her for the food, I asked her what drove her to start the restaurant. She replied, "My daughter is celiac and couldn't eat anywhere. I thought about how hard it must be for others. I desired to help them." What a beautiful motivating factor for helping others in pursuing a goal! Thinking back to another time I took a trip to Israel, I spoke to an olive tree farmer. He was passionate about reaping the best-tasting olive and learning the ins and outs of horticulture, nutrition, watering, and caretaking of these trees. His motivation? He wanted delectable olives for people to eat and use in soaps, medicines, and lotions. He wanted the best for the five-star restaurants that bought his olive oil and curing ailments and skin conditions in people. Another incredible motivation with purpose in life!

I once met two church pastors. The first became a pastor to follow in his dad's footsteps as a pastor. His words and intentions were different than his father's. He focused his words, actions, and motives on receiving donations and filling the church rather than caring and leading the people from a sincere heart. The second pastor led a preaching life because he loved people, was passionate about God's word and helping people understand it and had a serving heart—two vastly different motives and driving factors in life.

I've encountered a wealthy man and a poor man. The wealthy man had a drive to make money and do whatever it took to obtain it and still earn more. So much so that he hardly spent time with his wife and kids, working seven days a week. He was restless, stressed, and burned out with his relationship with his wife and kids. What was his motivation? He grew up poor and was afraid of being poor. He wanted to prove his worth to his neglectful father and a woman who rejected him in the past. The poor man said he was a successful man in finance at one point in his life. When he lost his wife and daughter in an accident, his life's objectives changed. He started to question life and its purpose despite having everything the world offers: a large house on the beach, an ample bank account, numerous toys, a successful career, and an expensive car. He said it was all an illusion and the American dream was a lie. He said he found more purpose and discovered more of himself in his newfound life, getting rid of all he had and living like a poor man.

    I recall two scenarios with women who desired to marry and have kids. Both accomplished their dreams in marriage and giving life to healthy children. The one's incentive was to prove to her abusive parents that she could be a better wife and parent than they were to her. The other woman was raised by loving, caring parents. She wanted a husband and children to tend to, love, and cherish. Both are vastly different reasons for reaching a goal in their life. With these scenarios, I'm giving examples of those with a life-sustaining purpose and those that could lead to destruction with a life-destructive purpose.

    Consider this: if you were to encounter four individuals. Two are wealthy, and two are poor. All of them say they are blessed. One of the poor and one of the wealthy say God blessed them. The other two do not acknowledge a creator at all. Isn't it safe to say that each finds purpose and sees various perspectives differently? Let's suppose that there were two different men; one was a professional sports player, while another was a restaurant worker. One prays to win the championship, and the other prays to be rich. Aren't both using God for the wrong motives? Let's also suppose two more individuals don't believe in God yet have the same life paths as those who believe in God. So then, what is the purpose of all these people? Who has discovered a greater path of living?

Chapter 2: Purpose With Peace

Making decisions about your life can involve many important areas, such as your education, career, spouse, house, car, where you live, and your travel plans. While making these choices can be challenging, it is an inevitable part of life. Since I was young, I have loved the beach, especially the tropical mountains. I've explored places like Hawaii and Costa Rica, where I met people living on the edge and constantly seeking their next adventure, escape, or getaway. People there surf, hang out with friends, party, smoke weed, relax, eat and drink, or have fun and let loose.

I met a gentleman who was a successful business owner and multimillionaire. I caught his attention because I shook his hand and treated him respectfully without knowing anything about him. He wanted to meet at a location where we would coincidentally arrive at the same time, hang out, and engage in something adventurous. He previously spent a few weeks in Japan, explored Indonesia for several more weeks, went snowboarding in the Rocky Mountains of Colorado, and was about to head to Central America for more exploring. Deep down, I've never found someone who is truly at peace or has found their purpose.

Many people are searching for "chill and cool vibes." However, they often feel a sense of uncertainty and are seeking deeper meaning in life. Despite this, they intensely desire adventure and wanderlust, longing to jump on a plane and explore new destinations, even if those experiences are temporary. Although this may provide temporary satisfaction, it lacks long-lasting purpose and peace. Like many others, I enjoy hiking in random places worldwide and discovering nature. I'll climb on rocks and trees, stare at the plants, catch lizards and snakes, walk barefoot, and relax in a stream, river, or body of water. I'll enjoy soaking up the sun's rays or engaging in risky and adventurous activities. Some thrilling pursuits I look forward to are sky diving, speedboat riding, fast car driving, ziplining, jet skiing, skiing, playing basketball, snorkeling, river rafting, go-karting, climbing a volcano, and even the opportunity to take a hot air balloon ride and float in the sky. I wanted to experience everything, get out of my comfort zone, and discover more about life without fear. In my youth, I was afraid of spiders, but now, as an adult, I overcame my fears and held a tarantula.

I learned to embrace spontaneous adventures and experiences, resulting in wonderful memories. Some shallow and closed-minded individuals pursue leisure and travel solely for pleasure. Whether boasting about the five-star hotel and resort they stayed at in Cancun, Mexico, sharing their experience of visiting the Eiffel Tower in Paris or discussing the wine they drank and the food they enjoyed, many people talk about similar tourist experiences. They often highlight the pampered service they received, the popular tourist spots visited, or the cruise they took to the same destinations as everyone else. Yet, who adventures beyond the tourist spots, discovering nature, engaging with people, and taking less traveled roads and paths? What is the heart's motivation for doing what you do? Or going where you decide to travel? What about living where you are? Some people know the answer, while others may not. Some may say, "Well, I saw pictures on social media, and it looks beautiful." While another may say, "It's a place I've always wanted to go." While another may say, "I'm not sure. I just want to go."

Whatever the reason or motivation, you have to ask the bigger question. "What is my reason, and how will this help me grow?" I have met people who moved to specific countries to become English teachers, but only for one or two years. They were seeking something deeper that aligns with their identity, as they were on a quest to discover meaning in life. People exploring their identities while seeking a more significant purpose through the many places I've been and the people I've talked to during my travels. I would ask them about their dream place they desire to go to in the world, and most have one common interest and desire: Bali, Indonesia. It's been voted one of the world's most beautiful places to visit, ranking number one in Asia. What about Bali grabs the interest of so many souls and allures their hearts and minds?

I sought out this question and discovered the answer for myself. I first realized that most of Indonesia is Muslim, but with Bali, it's Balinese Hinduism. Indonesia is a beautiful country with some regions of great wealth and luxury and others extreme poverty. Many people see the luxury of Bali and the enticing allurement advertised on social media by influencers, making this island appear like paradise. Isn't it interesting that there was once a Garden of Eden before the ecosystem changed and man burned with lust and desire for knowledge of right and wrong? Yet, even now, most humans still desire a tropical paradise garden with beautiful and serene, lush foliage. I couldn't help but notice the impoverished slums that existed in Bali. Remember I just mentioned the tourists who only visit areas frequented by other tourists? This perspective reflects humanity's common feelings and thoughts, but how many people are willing to care, desire, or passionately seek to learn more? How many have a deep longing to see and explore the aspects of life that most overlook or never take the time to discover? Bali is affordable for most, luxurious for many, and houses are fit for a king sitting amongst the foliage of the jungles and rainforests. Many homes are off the grid, providing an escape from the hustle and bustle of life and offering a serene, relaxing paradise feel.

I have also noticed that many people embrace Balinese Hindu spirituality. Although many say they don't follow a religion, they live according to what feels right to have inner peace. They believe in being true to yourself, caring for the environment, practicing self-love, loving others, respecting others, discovering enlightenment and self-discovery, and connecting with one's spirit, seeking liberation and harmony with nature, people, spirits, or gods and goddesses. I observed how many people practice yoga and meditation to pursue inner peace and enlightenment. They also believe sexuality is a natural part of life and seek to discover sexual enlightenment and freedom. I can understand how this can be so enticing and desirable for the flesh of a human. To live free, have no rules, and enjoy the world around you while being a good person from your perspective. The appeal of many of these women captivates men across the region and the world, igniting lust and desire for what some may view as forbidden, much like the tree in the Garden of Eden. I noticed their boyfriends or husbands follow the same patterns as women in these practices. Like Solomon, who is known as the wealthiest man to ever live with an estimated worth of $2.1 trillion, these individuals began adopting the spiritual practices and actions of women from various countries that intrigued them. How could this happen, and why?

There are shamans worldwide who sometimes have healing abilities, but the people they touch become more distressed and restless than before. Destinations like Ibiza and islands off the coast of Spain offer couples retreats designed to connect with their sexual energies. Even allowing their partners to touch other men or women while meditating together. Some women even practice tantra touch to explore their sexual energies. These actions were performed in ancient times as a rebellion against the God of Israel. This living is not peace, discovery, or the purpose of life. These actions reflect what the Bible warned against: causing death, suffering, sickness, wars, and the destruction of oneself and others in the world. It's the reason people had sex under Asherah polls, sought goddesses, burned incense to spirits, applied essential oils to connect with gods, sought idols made by human hands, and did whatever seemed right to them—burning with passions, desires, and cravings birthed within the human body and cravings of the flesh. Whenever ancient Israel or other nations practiced these behaviors, war, famine, sickness, and plague afflicted the land.

Let's take Pompeii, for example, burning with lust, seeking various gods and spirits, full of luxury, spas, prostitution, child sex, and orgies. Eventually, a volcano erupted, destroying the city and turning it to ashes as negative energy spread worldwide. At the same time, people believed that they were sending positive vibes and energy into the universe through their practices. These same practices are in Bali, Indonesia, and many places across the world, where people reject the Bible and react negatively to any discussion about it. True peace cannot be achieved without discovering the way, the truth, and the life. While Bali may seem like paradise, several lesser-known issues exist, such as over-tourism, traffic congestion, water scarcity, scams, price gouging, pollution, and the prevalence of garbage—including plastics and cans—washed up on the beaches.

Furthermore, a consistent fee is often associated with every activity you engage in. Take, for example, the popular tourist attraction featuring a swing amidst the rice fields, where visitors snap photos for social media. How many people are aware that the influence of others shapes their cravings, desires, choices, and life paths? Without these outer and inner influences, how many genuinely discover their purpose and path? Many desire to go to Bali, but what is truly within one's heart for longing for this endeavor in life? What about any desire that you have? What is directing that desire of longing within yourself? Is it your purpose, your destiny, and your plan for your life? Like Bali, many only see what everyone else sees and go where everyone else goes and desires what everyone else desires. But how many in life take the path few others take because your purpose calls for a greater purpose and plan beyond yourself waiting to be discovered? I have always believed anyone can visit the same places as others around the world. Many travel to the same countries, cities, restaurants, and attractions. However, the experiences are never identical; the steps, paths, and life imprints will always be unique to each individual. Just like your fingerprints and tongue, no two are the same. Similarly, your life's purpose is uniquely designed, just like your speech. It's up to you to discover a greater purpose for your life, unaffected by forces within the world.

> "Although this may provide temporary satisfaction, it lacks long-lasting purpose and peace." *-Todd Aaron*

Chapter 3: My Purpose Sought Purpose Lost

We have two roads that we can take in life. One has a great purpose beyond ourselves, while the other represents the purpose of the world. At multiple points in my life, I had to distance myself from everyone and everything. Each time an earthquake occurred, it led me to reevaluate the foundation's structural integrity upon which I built my life. As a child, I watched children's movies and believed I would become something great someday. My parents and strangers always told me I was smart and intelligent. I have a genius IQ and ranked in the top 1% globally for spatial intelligence. At the age of seven, I completed a five thousand-piece puzzle. I invented various things, took apart and reassembled numerous items, and solved adult-level crossword puzzles and mazes. I loved "I Spy" and Seek and Find books. I wrote a children's book, which a teacher and writer published. I coded websites, made graphic designs before age 10, and helped teach adults audio, video, and PowerPoint in a congregation while memorizing more verses in the Bible than anyone has ever seen. In 2nd and 3rd grade, I ranked nationally in testing as a 6th and 7th grader. Still, I was being shaped and molded into an image of someone I did not know.

For example, schools often hold career days where students are asked what they want to be when they grow up. During these events, adults from various occupations come to the school to discuss their careers. They are shaping you and preparing you for a career, just as the school prepares you to be an efficient and obedient worker in society. Or should I say, an obedient slave to a system designed by man? After all, schools and colleges were created to enlarge the workload and teach people to be better workers to increase greedy business profits.

I wanted to pursue careers as a musician, architect, videographer, or astronomer. As I grew older and began making music and performing shows, I had the opportunity to open for many Billboard-charting musicians and even appeared on TV and radio. However, despite all the attention and success I experienced, I felt a strong inner pull and a deep stirring that urged me to step away from it all. I resisted the temptations of drugs, alcohol, and sleeping around with women, which most celebrities were, and many encouraged me to do. The influence and the peer pressures were weighty, but I believed something greater than I was protecting me.

I experienced a major revelation when I realized that my dreams and goals stemmed from feelings of betrayal and neglect during my childhood. I experienced physical, sexual, emotional, spiritual, and religious abuse. The negativity from those who didn't support me fueled my desire to succeed. I felt driven to prove them wrong, to show my parents—who divorced when I was ten—that I could become something great. I wanted to demonstrate to others who felt broken like me that it was possible to achieve something remarkable. It wasn't until I started feeling incredibly off that I began questioning my reality. I recall standing in a nightclub as I opened for a billboard-charting musician when something happened inside me. I stand there, watching over two thousand fans screaming and losing their minds for a celebrity who was intoxicated and under the influence as I help support him. Young women screaming, pushing through security to touch a piece of his clothes. He claimed success, wealth, and everything he could ever want. However, something deep within me made me feel sick and disgusted.

    I grew up in a mixed-religion household and was aware of God's laws, but I never fully understood who Jesus was. This mix led me to question many things, mainly how I ended up where I am now. Why am I doing this? Who am I? Is this worth it? I began getting curious and felt like something was missing. I came across a Messianic Jewish rabbi, which sparked my interest. About fifteen years ago, I started hearing about Greg Hershberg, a Messianic Jewish rabbi from the Bronx, New York. At that moment, I found a greater purpose with Yeshua, Jesus the Messiah. I cried out that night and asked if this Yeshua was real. He revealed himself to me and delivered me from all my sins while I was prostrated in the shower, crying out in anguish with my entire being. My heart, soul, and mind cried out in a way I had never experienced before. Jesus gave me incredible peace, love, and joy. I was instantly delivered from all my sins and unforgiveness.

    I deleted phone numbers and removed myself from the music entertainment scene. I left behind everything I had been pursuing and gave up my achievements for this new life I discovered. I embarked on a journey of greater purpose, dedicating myself to studying the Gospels extensively, with a particular focus on the New Testament. I was already familiar with the Old Testament. I saw the correlation between the Old and New Testaments as I read more of the Bible. They came to life in a way I had never experienced before. I put a lot of effort into my studies and prayed earnestly with God before I began evangelizing. I had been diagnosed with chronic Lyme disease, Bartonella, and Babesia, all as a result of a tick bite. I nearly died from Lyme disease, which I didn't know I had. This financial hardship and suffering changed my perspective on life and others more than ever before. It drove me to pursue a new and different path in my life. However, I discovered a greater purpose in sharing the good news and what I learned.

The demand and attention overwhelmed me as an evangelist, social media influencer, and pastor. I was burdened by having millions of views on my content and thousands of followers. I preached in prisons, churches, and streets to gang members, murderers, prostitutes, Satanists, Hindus, drug addicts, Muslims, Jews, Christians, new-agers, witches, and many others. I saw people healed from sickness and chronic illness to physical ailments and disabilities, delivered from addictions, alcohol, porn, and much more. I witnessed marriages and families restored, and hearts changed with compassion and love. A new birth of hope from the lives of many, in which God used a simple man like myself as a vessel, all for his glory and purpose.

Unfortunately, I received too much attention, some good and some bad. I was becoming too popular while preaching. Souls were instantly delivered from every sin, addiction, and struggle known to humanity as God's power moved into their lives. At the same time, mega-churches, leaders, and pastors from popular chain churches across Australia and America—including cities like Atlanta, Los Angeles, Dallas, and Seattle—began to express their anger toward the messages I shared. These messages focused on topics such as sin, repentance, and holy living and included criticism of Kanye West. The churches began to worship him, play his music, and advertise his shows. In my zeal and love to protect people, I later realized something God showed me. I read it thousands of times before but have never fully understood it until now. God says in Matthew 13:24-30 not to pull up the tares, or else you might pull up the wheat with it, and to let them grow together until the harvest. I realized that I must let them be and focus on my purpose.

Later, I dealt with betrayal from some close to me, had terrible things done to me, and had many defamations and spread lies about me.

I once again felt like I was losing myself despite having multiple supporters. I prayed about it and heard God tell me to "leave social media and get alone with me." I obeyed and once again deleted phone numbers and apps, distancing myself from the world. I explored, advertised, isolated, and slowed down like never before. A quote from Evangelist Leonard Ravenhill rang in my ears.

"Man of God, if you can get alone for three years, stay there."

I obeyed right after seeking a greater purpose for my life. During those three years, I went through hell on earth seeking therapy, much like I did during my teenage years amidst my parents' divorce. I had a severe traumatic experience that resulted in intense PTSD, which uncovered childhood fears I didn't realize I had. During various stages of my recovery, I traveled to the Rocky Mountains in the United States, the Carpathian Mountains in Romania, and the Swiss Alps in Slovenia, Austria, and Switzerland, experiencing ups and downs. I was hearing lies and voices from the devil telling me that I was worthless, defeated, going to hell, God didn't love me, and to kill myself. During these moments, I sought more profound help from pastors in the faith for thirty to fifty years. All of these told me that they went through a period in their life where they went through the same trials as me during ministry. That was reassuring, yet how long would this remain? What was this purpose? Why do I feel like God has abandoned me, even though he promises, "I'll never leave you nor forsake you?"

I reflected on the purpose I had envisioned as a child and teenager, which eventually faded away. I later found a new purpose, but that, too, disappeared. Once again, I discovered a sense of purpose, only to have it redirected yet again. I had a full-fledged ministry to care for, a wife and children, and people who needed my help. However, I realized that I needed to step back to help myself, but I found it challenging to do so. Who could help me? What could be done? Someone once said, "Man's plans are like garbage cans." It took me an exceptionally long time to finally understand what that meant.

I remember driving through the Carpathian Mountains on a road that was voted the most beautiful road in the world. The radar map showed thick cloud formations covering the country and surrounding areas. It was disappointing because the fog obscured all the natural beauty. I was with my brother, silently praying to God in the dense clouds and fog, where visibility was less than the length of a car. I asked God to show me His beauty so that I could glorify His name for the work of His hands. I requested that He build my faith and grant us grace and favor. In response, I heard His voice say, "Five more miles." As we drove five more miles, the beauty of God's creation became clear before us. At that moment, I realized that our will and timing are not our own. However, when we focus on God, everything in our lives and paths becomes clear. I remember a verse in the Bible that states, "We must go through many hardships to enter the kingdom of God." The road can become unclear and foggy when we dictate to God how we should live or convince ourselves of what we believe is our purpose. The reality is that there is so much more for us to learn as we seek to discover our true purpose.

I almost started a business with many clients lined up, all eager to work with me and encouraging my efforts. I developed and perfected a technology that could have made me millions of dollars, and many people wanted to use it without hesitation. But what would I have lost? Myself, my wife, and my children. I didn't recognize it then, but later in life, I understood the greater purpose behind my experiences. I was so caught up in the busyness of life that I almost lost sight of the meaningful journey ahead. Once again, God protected me as He had in the music industry, ministry, and throughout my life.

I began to ask myself, "What is my purpose, and what is the purpose of life for humanity?" I realized that I no longer craved leadership, attention, or greatness or had any specific plans. I reflected on what had occurred in my life and wondered where it would lead me. I discovered that very few people truly understand their purpose or are willing to be patient, change, and remain humble as life shifts, much like the tides influenced by the wind and the moon. We must be adaptable and open to change for a greater purpose. The goal is not to resist the waves that life brings but to navigate them with peace, allowing them to guide us wherever they may take us.

> "Once things start to control us, we take our focus off the One who should be controlling us."
> — *Rabbi Greg Hershberg, A Life for God: A Rabbi's Analysis of Life, the Cross, and Eternity*

Chapter 4: Motivations of Purpose

You have two options before you. You may have already discovered one; the other is waiting to be explored. Which path will capture your interest? One leads to life, and the other leads to death. Everyone seeks peace, whether in the form of world peace, personal relationships, job satisfaction, environmental harmony, or inner tranquility. Many people find comfort in massages, vacations, spas, soothing music, nature, and the sounds of ocean waves. Others seek spiritual retreats, yoga, self-help books, meditation, therapy, and various forms of spiritual practice. Yet, at the end of this journey, many still yearn for another path. Deep down, they may still be restless at night, searching for greater peace and purpose. Some individuals pursue more money and job security, while others may give up on these pursuits, living paycheck to paycheck or even choosing a life without a permanent home. Each person's purpose is defined differently in their mind.

While traveling abroad and reflecting on my past travels, I sought to understand, observe, analyze, and gain wisdom about people, cultures, religions, societies, and how the world works. They all have one thing in common. They all desire peace, although their definition of obtaining peace differs. The most frequent prayer I've encountered from people, including requests, is for health and financial stability. To some, this is peace, while to others, it brings more destruction. From the luxurious penthouse suites, exotic island homes, and fast sports cars in Dubai to the slums of the Philippines, Africa, Thailand, and India—where the concept of luxury is almost unknown—there is a stark contrast in living conditions. In wealthy areas like Dubai, some of the greatest chefs prepare exquisite meals, while just behind the towering skyscrapers lie impoverished communities struggling with inadequate food and basic pleasures. Everywhere I've traveled, I've observed luxurious and lovely buildings and housing right next to poor buildings. What does purpose look like within both of these lifestyles?

I've experienced both sides of the spectrum growing up. I went from living in a mansion in a safe neighborhood to residing in a small apartment in a dangerous and impoverished area. Some people aspire to own a mansion and lead luxurious lives filled with shopping, pampering, and showcasing their success through cars, clothing, jewelry, hairstyles, fine dining, and overall living standards. But what happens once they achieve this lifestyle? What happens if one obtains this and then loses it?

I once knew a man who worked his life away to retire in Florida. When he finally retired, he only spent two weeks enjoying his secluded beach house until he suddenly died of a heart attack. Throughout all my travels, I have rarely met a wealthy person willing to listen when discussing God. Only a few people out of the thousands I've spoken to genuinely hold a clear belief in God. Some claim to believe, but upon further discussion, it becomes evident that their beliefs are a mix of elements drawn from various deities and religions. Money is often their god, as many believe in manifesting and visualizing money and riches to achieve their goals and dreams. This is the same temptation that the devil presented to Jesus. He showed Jesus all the riches and power of the world, offering riches in exchange for bowing down and worshiping him.

Many people around the world claim that once they become rich, they will do great things for others. However, they often don't realize that such a lifestyle can lead to more destruction. Take, for instance, the poor widow who gave her last coin in the temple courtyard in the Bible. While everyone else focused on the contributions of the wealthy Pharisees, who gave to be praised by others, this widow's offering was much more significant. Doesn't the same thing happen today with donations to nonprofits and organizations, especially when they are showcased on social media or news stations? Regardless of someone's economic situation, anyone can start being a good steward of what they have now. I have experienced being fed meals by people who were financially poor, living in homes with dirt floors and tin roofs. They offered their best to feed me and others, even when they had very little. They were grateful for the gospel message they received, the new life discovered, and the people they encountered. In contrast, when I've been fed by the wealthy, it has often come with ulterior motives—either an expectation to engage in their interests or a desire to gain something in return. Proverbs warns us about this when it says, "Do not desire his delicacies, for they are deceptive food."

People should reflect on why they crave certain things or desire what others have. Jesus said, "It is easier for a camel to go through the eye of a needle than for a rich man to enter the kingdom of heaven." This statement underscores the innocence and humility of individuals who remain like little children. Jesus also said, "Truly, I tell you, unless you change and become like little children, you will never enter the kingdom of heaven." Children are often eager to learn and receive what is told to them, while adults tend to be filled with opinions, emotions, and beliefs that can cloud their understanding. Jesus encouraged us to invite the poor, the crippled, the lame, and the blind to our banquets, assuring us that God will reward those who invite others who cannot repay them.

Some quote that "karma" is what you put out in the world and that the universe will return it to you. However, God spoke of these principles long before other ideologies formed around them. This brings us back to what engrains certain beliefs within the human soul, much like the ancient hieroglyphs inscribed on the walls of Egyptian pyramids.

The meals I've shared with those who have little have been among the greatest of my life. I've had more fulfilling experiences with families where a little child clutches a bag of rice in their modest home than dining high atop a skyscraper in a fancy restaurant. I have discovered more love and care from people with little but enormous hearts than those who are materially wealthy but emotionally disconnected.

Proverbs states, "It is better to be of a lowly spirit with the poor than to divide the spoil with the proud." I've found this to be true. Some people seek the praises of others, relishing compliments like "great job" or "well done." But how many seek affirmation from within or from a higher power, knowing they are fulfilling their life's calling and living true to themselves and their creator? How can one truly know they are living according to their purpose, especially a purpose not designed or influenced by others? As we continue this journey of discovering purpose, I realize that I find more fulfillment lying in a hammock, enjoying the sway of palm trees beside the beach, gazing at nature than visiting any shopping center, car dealership, mansion, or penthouse.

There is a saying that the more you have, the more unhappy you become, filled with worries. I have found this to ring true. My fondest memories are rooted in nature rather than in bustling cities. The unhappiest nations tend to be those with high levels of consumerism and overwork. Those focused on excessive shopping and accumulating wealth are often the most depressed and anxious. Even those who acquire riches without hard work can feel just as stressed as those striving to attain wealth.

Why is this the case? Because there are two sides to a coin. One side represents the desire to achieve goals and attain riches, while the other represents the fear of losing what one has gained. Individuals may build investments and substantial savings, but these are not secure, regardless of innovative money management.

Ultimately, no one is guaranteed tomorrow. Every human being will eventually die. Few strive to confront this reality and often run from it. However, if we need emergency surgery or become sick, we run to the doctor or a hospital to live. Most humans have a desire to live, while others seek to escape the stress of living. Nevertheless, we instinctively want to live and know there is another life after this one. Everyone will be part of a funeral, and deep down, this uncertainty is ingrained in the human soul as we seek understanding and purpose in our lives.

Many people ignore death and continue to pursue various pursuits in the world because they have yet to fulfill their greatest purpose or discover it. That is why humans across the Earth are still seeking more and desiring to achieve and obtain more. Every person alive should question, "Why am I doing what I'm doing? Why am I desiring the wants I have in life? Why am I living the way I am, or desiring to live a certain way? What are my dreams and goals, and what fuels them? Where did all this begin?"

Chapter 5: Discovering Purpose

Throughout my life, I have sought to understand the most significant question of existence. Some people rely on the Internet, news, media, religions, movies, social media, documentaries, other people's experiences, books, politicians, pictures, and more to acquire knowledge. But is this a reliable means of answering life's biggest questions like "What is my life's purpose?" It's a comprehensive, deep, and open-ended question. Many will have a typical vague response when asked that question, while others will respond with a more in-depth, intellectual answer. Regardless of what others believe in life, what is your purpose?

I have moved frequently and traveled extensively. Many people would look at me strangely or put me down when I chose not to settle in one city, buy a house, or pursue a conventional lifestyle with a single job. I've always had an unquenchable desire for adventure, figuring things out, solving problems, and unraveling mysteries. People often described me as spontaneous and random, but I realized I was far from average when discussing life's purpose.

Living in America, I often encounter questions like, "What do you do for a living? Where do you live? Where did you go to school? What degree did you obtain?" Being from America attracted the attention of others. Within the country, it is common for people to ask questions that assess one's financial status, such as, "What neighborhood do you live in? Where do you work? How many bedrooms and bathrooms does your house have? What kind of car do you drive? How much do you earn in a year?" Most of these questions appear normal with conversation, but how many ask questions that have nothing to do with one's net worth or financial status in the world? To many, this is a common appeal and interest.

These qualities are often sought within one's heart, especially when determining who another person is and if they are worth their time. In the same way, a sports fanatic compares players' stats on a sports team to the stats of other players or teams. The human mind often analyzes other humans through a lens of physical and worldly viewpoints implanted within the world's glasses rather than the lens of the spirit and soul uncorrupted by the world.

I often think about my endeavors in foreign countries in remote jungles or isolated villages that most Americans will never visit. The young and the old would often stare at me, but when I waved or spoke to them, they were incredibly friendly and welcoming. Not once did any of those individuals inquire about my financial status, job, education, career, house, car, or money. They were genuinely interested in my heart and wanted to hear the words that came from my mouth. With great curiosity, they asked questions that were uncommon for most people. The more I traveled, the more I helped people with humanitarian efforts, and the more I observed, experienced, and analyzed in this world. The more my curiosity and hunger grew in wisdom, understanding, and knowledge of how the world works and operates, the stronger my purpose of life began to grow.

I knew that man's pursuits, including my own, were a reflection of some past reality that the factory system of the world had fabricated. We have all been programmed, changed, and built to pursue the goals and dreams of someone greater than us. Coded within our minds and hearts is a desire to pursue something that many deem original and unique but is, in fact, a product of another, like someone who's been stamped with Made In China. Indeed, there is more to life beyond the sandy beaches, islands, and coastal regions. Something extraordinary than the Swiss Alps, Patagonia mountains in Chile, the Rocky Mountains of America and Canada, and the Himalayan Mountain Range. Something greater than the Sahara Desert and all its vast sand dunes and glory. Even greater than the incredible history and architecture of Europe made by man with tremendous awe and amazement. It is more beautiful than the snowy regions, jungles, or wildernesses worldwide. I look at the stars and know there is something greater than what man can fathom beyond our world.

As I traveled to various places, I noticed that nature throughout the world often looked quite similar. The main differences lie in the people, religion, food, cultures, and architecture of each location. I noticed that people's motivations for work differ significantly. In remote regions, some rely on fishing or hunting for survival, while in more populated areas, others work to earn more or enhance their enjoyment of life.

Some work for family, travel, a house, or some future goal. Others work to shop and buy more material possessions. I noticed how deeply ingrained consumerism has permeated cultures in many first-world countries, such as America. Many in other nations like Europe have described Americans as shallow and superficial. Americans and first-world countries are loud in restaurants and often haughty or prideful. Many who move to America lose their sense of self, while those living within its borders often exhibit a sense of entitlement and pride.

Though I love America, it has vastly changed since the removal of God, individuality, purpose, and morality from schools. Our society and the government have been exponentially impacted. Sadly, the common discussions are about jobs, money, restaurants, entertainment, shows, movies, shopping, sports, or the winery or bar experience they had during a vacation. The more meaningful discussions are rarely addressed, as if people find them unpleasant or bitter. Many have a low tolerance for deep conversations, resembling a tendency to swipe away interactions as one does on TikTok in search of the next quick visual or mental stimulation.

In some countries, I have discussed the Bible or God in general. Many people ask questions out of curiosity. In contrast, in America, it's increasingly common to see expressions on faces as if they have smelled poop, showing distaste and no interest. It's a sad reality as morals and values are declining, and the characteristics that made humankind so beautiful are crumbling at the foundation of consumerism and the pursuit of self and wealth. In the early 1930s-1960s, God, neighbors, community, education, and church were some of the most engaged in activities. In today's society, our top engagements are social media, cell phones, TV, education, sports, and entertainment. It's as if Rome is once again entertaining the masses in the Colosseum. Antiochus and the Greeks did this in ancient Israel to distract the people from family and God and corrupt their morals and values. Maybe that's why sports and entertainment venues have male designs with the same oval and stadium seating. The phrase "There is nothing new under the sun," as quoted by Solomon, raises an intriguing question.

My point is that many people have lost their sense of self. Although they believe they have control over their lives and understand their direction, we need to ask ourselves what is truly valuable to each of us. Each year, profits rise in various sectors such as Hollywood, sports, movies, storage units, retail sales, car sales, real estate, entertainment shows, car washes, phones, churches, movie theaters, restaurants, electronics, and more. The population has clearly expressed its priorities. Is this what life is all about? Is this truly the purpose of life?

I visited the Tomb of Jesus in Israel without being part of a tour group. While I was there, a man from Texas who was part of a church tour group initiated a conversation with me. He asked where I was from, what I did for a living, and other questions about my occupation, seemingly trying to gauge my financial status. As I said before, this type of questioning is quite common in America. I was beginning to feel irritated, but just before it was my turn to enter the tomb, I took a moment to appreciate the experience with God. He mentioned, "I know a very rich man in your industry and one has a massive house, nice cars, and a lot of money, he's doing well for himself." I cut him off, said, "excuse me," and walked away.

This mentality is a problem for many regions with access to material wealth. They can stand at the tomb of Jesus yet still fail to recognize His glory and presence, often lacking a focus on His kingdom and what truly matters. In Europe, I frequently encountered people with a healthier work-life balance, paying less attention to material gain. In their free time, they indulge in massages, get haircuts, visit spas, and travel for leisure or personal enjoyment. While many aspire to live life to the fullest, many overlook the importance of God. This neglect is often linked to views related to Communism and can be perceived as a loss of freedom. It's no wonder that it's one of the highest provinces for consumerist smoking, alcohol, prostitution, live music, restaurant dining, and partying. Although it's common to see people enjoying a cup of coffee during their day and conversing with someone else or others for two to three hours, they often smoke and don't want to speak about religion, politics, or God, as it kills their vibe.

In their view, God has become more of a cultural or family tradition and a political burden rather than a love, joy, and treasure. Some, such as those in Eastern Europe, believe their religion is a more moral and social rebellion against the more relaxed and declining morals of the West and a family tradition. Many correlate it to Communism through the rituals of church attendance and would rather live a free life. Nevertheless, it's easy to talk to doctors, lawyers, judges, and business owners in those countries with deep intellectual conversations without feeling judged. However, in first-world countries like America, Australia, the United Kingdom, and Canada, you rarely engage in purposeful conversations, especially without judgment on your social or economic status.

Even with all our conversations and interactions about life, it is rare for anyone to genuinely answer the question of life's purpose without repeating something already said by the world or others. A true, life-driven purpose is often beyond what the average person can see.

I once spoke to a man who retired to a beach house on an island. He had previously worked as a crane operator in Atlantic City, building casinos. He claimed to have discovered the purpose of life in his old age, yet he still struggled with depression and loneliness. I also met a retired lawyer in his eighties who asserted that he had figured out life and God. He talked about finding his purpose, yet he still adhered to a biblical message centered on prosperity and wealth. Another man I encountered owned a large house and dozens of chain restaurants. He claimed to have found life's purpose while continually seeking more wealth and drinking alcohol frequently. I met a woman who had overcome cancer but was battling it again while raising her daughter and caring for her husband. She also spoke of having discovered the meaning of life.

Another man on the island of Socotra lives in a cave with no modern amenities or possessions. He simply fishes, cooks it himself, enjoys life, and says, "I'm happy in life." When asked, "Why?" He responds, "Me and the people here are happy because of the goats, rain that falls, and the grass that grows." He also mentioned God and the ocean. What was it that this man discovered that is considered rare or odd in the modern world?

Then, there was a woman I knew who was dying from cancer. She found hope through my preaching and messages. She had two daughters and a husband, and despite her illness, she prayed incessantly, read the Bible constantly, and cared for her loving family. She began sharing God's love and forgiveness with doctors and nurses. Before she passed away, she wrote a message on her mirror, which was the last picture she had taken. It read, "The closer it comes, the more clearly I see." That night, she passed away with a Bible on her bathroom counter. The purpose of life is often not found in the living but instead discovered in facing death. However, not everyone nearing death gains this clarity. Many have near-death experiences but continue to live as they always have. Only those who begin to question their lives, seek greater purpose and meaning, and desire true freedom can discover life's ultimate purpose.

"It's a sad reality as morals and values are declining, and the characteristics that made humankind so beautiful are crumbling at the foundation of consumerism and the pursuit of self and wealth." *-Todd Aaron*

Chapter 6: Purpose Beyond Life

Bronnie Ware, a nurse, highlights in her book the most common regrets expressed by people as they approach the end of their lives. These regrets are:

1. They wished they had the courage to live a life true to themselves rather than the life others expected of them.
2. They wished they didn't work so hard.
3. They wished they had the courage to express their feelings.
4. They wished they stayed in touch with their friends.
5. They wished they had allowed themselves to be happier.

These are all intriguing regrets from individuals who believe they have discovered their purpose.

[Bronnie Ware. (2012). The Top 5 Regrets of the Dying: A Life Transformed by the Dearly Departing. Hay House.]

I have heard many interesting regrets from older adults about what they would do differently if they could live their lives over again. Here are some key reflections:

1. They would work less and focus less on making and saving money.
2. They would have spent more time with their children.
3. They would have loved and cherished their spouse more and enjoyed more fun together.
4. They would have adventured out and explored the world more.
5. They would not have tolerated or remained in unfulfilling jobs and companies.
6. They would have forgiven more and been less angry over minor matters.
7. They would have prayed more and lived in greater accordance with their faith in God.

These thoughts from many individuals at the end of their lives are fascinating. People who once thought they had found a meaningful purpose are now piecing together their experiences and assessing the bigger picture of their lives as a whole.

I've never met a man over eighty or ninety who wished he had worked more. Every person I have spoken to wishes they had spent more time with family and less time working. Some have expressed these deep pains with tears and sadness as they realized time flew by. Every single one would tell me, "Don't blink."

When my daughter was born over a decade ago, an elderly man told me, "They grow up fast. Take as many videos and pictures as you can. Don't blink." I took his advice, but I didn't fully understand it at the time. Now, I see grown men expressing how they couldn't wait for their children to grow up and leave the house. They are now in tears, lamenting their homes' quietness and their children's absence. After years of being incredibly busy, I am grateful for the time I can now spend resting with my youngest daughter. We read books together, pray, hold each other, take naps, and enjoy walks while I hold her tiny hand. I have heard many sad men regret not being able to engage in these simple activities because they were too preoccupied with work, the pursuit of success, and various hobbies. Many believe that if they start a business, become famous, or gain wealth, they will suddenly have more freedom and time to spend with their family. This idea is one of the biggest lies ever perpetrated by humanity.

I've noticed that many celebrities, business owners, and wealthy individuals spend less time with their families and more time focused on work, money, and social engagements. For instance, I know a doctor who owns an integrative medical practice; he and his wife must put their children in daycare because they are both busy managing the business. They rarely have time for vacations or quality family moments, so they hardly spend time together as a couple. Both appear severely depressed.

Unfortunately, this is the reality for many of those in high social or economic positions. Numerous celebrities rely on others to care for their children, while many affluent individuals are so preoccupied with their pursuits that they neglect their children's emotional, mental, or moral needs. Although they can provide for their family's physical needs — such as education, housing, and financial support — this is only a tiny part of being a parent. As I mentioned in the first chapter, these neglected children often grow up following in their parents' confused and lost footsteps. Others may rebel, turning to drugs, partying, promiscuity, or even engaging in prostitution. They often find themselves spiraling into a pit of despair due to neglect and a lack of love.

I have met many parents who believe that financial support, a good education, a car, and resources for a successful future equate to love. For example, I once met a man whose father owned much of a large town in Texas. Despite his wealth, the man's character, kindness, morals, values, respect, and care for others were utterly absent from his heart and mind. He was the manager of a large company. His dad bought him a large house and big trucks, yet he treated everyone like slaves and garbage. He had a big ego full of pride, hatred, and darkness. I noticed his wife's body language and observed his children. All were well cared for and pampered, yet they appeared miserable and hollow inside. I have seen this in many families. They often hide behind a mask of flaunting material possessions, social outings, sports, shopping, leisure travels, dining out, parties, alcohol, achievements, and enjoyable experiences. This attitude is how they conceal their pain and lack of purpose. Unfortunately, few will escape the suffocating grip of this emptiness, which is draining the life out of so many before it's too late.

I have seen many women who enter marriage believing it will resemble a Disney "happily ever after" story. They are often mesmerized and infatuated with their partner, convinced that the person is perfect and can do no wrong. This outlook leads them to eagerly anticipate an incredible wedding and a wonderful life ahead. However, I have observed that the "honeymoon phase" tends to be short-lived, lasting only two to three years, as dopamine, endorphins, oxytocin, and serotonin levels begin to decline. As time passes, these individuals may find fault in their partner over trivial matters, such as "you left the toilet seat up" or "your hair is everywhere." The fantasy life they once envisioned begins to fade. Although having pets or children can reignite some of those feel-good hormones and foster bonding, this spark often diminishes again after some time following the child's birth. Statistically, many divorces occur within the first seven years of marriage, particularly during the first four years of a child's life. In wealthy countries like America, this translates to approximately 1 in 2 marriages ending in divorce. The statistics are even higher for those whose weddings cost over $1,000 and a further increase for marriages with weddings over $20,000, and even where the wedding ring costs between $2,000 and $4,000.

Many women mentioned in the statistics above seem more likely to seek more entertainment, shopping, travel, dining experiences, and social media attention. Additionally, I have observed many of them engaging with self-help literature or consuming fantasy, promiscuous, sexual, or violent domination novels and films. What can we gather from this behavior? The purpose and goals that one aspires to in life could be a fantasy designed and shaped by societal influences. Many people yearn for that ideal "happily ever after" experience.

I've seen a pattern in marriages where a woman seeks a successful, wealthy man. Initially, she ends up with someone who treats her with respect. He will put on and remove her jacket at a restaurant, pull out and push in her chair, and open and close doors for her. He buys her sweet gifts, does kind things, and shows her respect and good manners. However, as time goes on, he stops being the gentleman and prince who once swept her off her feet. How could this happen?

The purpose and goals that society promotes are often based on a worldly framework created by human minds rather than on life-sustaining purposes such as peace and happiness. Many marriages falter because they do not truly honor the vows of "for better or for worse." When they become faced with difficulties such as financial struggles, chronic illness, injury, paralysis, long-term job loss, or losing possessions, how many couples genuinely love each other enough to stick together until "death do them part?" A deeper connection must bind them beyond what the world can offer.

Many women seek a partner who treats them like royalty while simultaneously desiring wealth and material possessions. However, as God says, "You cannot love God and money," you can't have both. The chance of finding someone who genuinely lives for God, treats you with love and respect, does not idolize money, and is financially stable is less than 0.01%. You must decide what is most valuable to you and understand why you desire the things you do in life.

For those who own businesses or seek to climb the corporate ladder for prestigious positions, what drives your pursuit? What drives those souls within humans to reach those goals? I often tell people that the higher you ascend in your career, the more stress and responsibility you will encounter. Many find it leads to less freedom, increased demands, and limited time. For entrepreneurs, the reality is that the more time you invest in your business, the more worries you'll face. The common misconception is that success will grant them greater freedom and independence, but this, too, is misleading.

I've met many individuals who idolize fame and long for its qualities, yet they often overlook the realities that come with it. It can seem like a glamorous rose garden, but the thorns can cause pain once you immerse yourself in it. Consider how many celebrities enter rehab, go through divorces, or struggle with mental health issues. Many are forced to hire private security or can't enjoy a meal out without being hounded for photos. Is this honestly considered a purpose-driven life?

Some individuals who faced rejection and neglect in childhood may crave attention and praise from others. However, they often find that achieving fame leads to greater feelings of emptiness, loneliness, and unhappiness. They may discover that the true, fulfilling life they yearn for remains elusive, even when they hit rock bottom. It is easy to escape from one's purpose and ignore the profound and often dark realities buried within. Yet, finding the help you need to uncover your true self and purpose can be incredibly challenging.

People typically gravitate toward the familiar instead of the unknown. They might prioritize convenience, opting for junk food over healthy options, rather than nurturing their souls with steadfast purpose. I frequently encounter individuals who claim their purpose is to "be yourself, achieve your passions, leave a legacy, find happiness and fulfillment, focus on personal growth, discover spirituality, and be true to who you are." While this mindset can inspire motivational speeches and bestselling books, it does not encapsulate the ultimate purpose of life. Deep down, many who express such opinions still search for a greater purpose, often surrendering to a limited understanding and saying, "What I have discovered is a better purpose than what I previously knew." However, this acknowledgment usually does not satisfy their ongoing quest for deeper meaning. This inner longing drives people to pursue relaxation and spiritual retreats, vacations, yoga, meditation, and other escapes as they seek one meaningful experience after another. You may enjoy a massage or spa treatment, which is perfectly fine, but it will only provide temporary relaxation. It lasts only as long as the treatment itself. Once that time is over, the stress relief fades, and the desire for more returns. Is this the reality for those who believe they are on a path to finding purpose yet remain stuck in this cycle? One can read every self-help book, attend guided meditations, experience spiritual enlightenment, and undergo countless counseling and therapy sessions. Yet, when they lay their heads on their pillows at night and close their eyes, they may still feel something is missing.

One may quickly respond, "No, that's not true!" This reaction often stems from being satisfied with their current condition. It is not until one contemplates what comes after this life and questions reality that one begins to see life's true colors. Indeed, there is a creator and something greater than ourselves—someone who can help us heal from trauma, pain, hurt, depression, fear, worry, PTSD, and the chaos of our lives. Consider a car with all its parts, including the engine and electrical components, that were taken apart and left in a garage. How could it put itself back together without a builder? Similarly, if you have all the ingredients for a recipe in your kitchen, can the dish prepare itself without someone to cook it? Of course not!

Therefore, a great designer must have created every substance we use to build things on this earth, yet few will ever truly seek out this truth. Let alone question how everything—from the brain and heart to DNA and every living cell—is intricately purposed and designed with intelligent intent.

Chapter 7: Freedom With Purpose

I have traveled to many places, learning about various cultural practices, religions, lifestyles, and beliefs. Throughout my journey, I came to understand that there is one true freedom, healing, and purpose in life. Since the dawn of creation, people have sought after many gods and spiritual experiences, longing for a greater purpose and a sense of belonging in this world. One significant observation I have made is the source of hope, purpose, peace, healing, joy, happiness, love, and comfort that people often overlook or reject. It is a topic that many hesitate to discuss, shunning or even becoming angry at the very mention of it.

I've preached in prisons where individuals have been sentenced to 15 years to life. In those settings, I witnessed some of the most powerful moves of God and meaningful spiritual experiences. It's remarkable how, even in such desperate circumstances, murderers and gang members found themselves on their hands and knees, crying out in anguish with tears streaming down on the cold concrete floor while I and others prayed for them with love and care. How is it that when they finally stood up, there was a new countenance and light in their eyes? This spiritual change is something that I have seen all too often. Many of these individuals have been disillusioned by church, religion, or God. Yet, deep within their beings, something stirs in the innermost regions of their souls. It's a cry that seems to echo throughout the universe, rippling through time and into eternity—a cry filled with regret, sadness, and a longing for mercy and forgiveness.

Something greater than themselves shows up and transforms their heart, soul, and mind. A verse which rings clear from the Bible, "A new heart also will I give you, and a new spirit will I put within you; and I will take away the stony heart out of your flesh, and I will give you a heart of flesh. And I will put my Spirit within you, and cause you to walk in my statutes, and you shall keep mine ordinances, and do them." How can this be?

We all have a lawless nature, though expressed in different ways. Suddenly, these individuals experience new desires, feelings, and longings, accompanied by a newfound love! Many have described this moment by saying, "I have never felt like this before!" It's a moment of overwhelming joy and tears—pure happiness. I've seen an elderly woman, upon hearing one simple message, exclaim, "I've been going to church my whole life and have heard thousands of sermons, yet I feel different as if I'm a child once again."

I think about the words of Yeshua (Jesus the Messiah), who said, "Very truly I tell you, no one can see the kingdom of God unless they are born again." How is this possible?

I have witnessed this transformation in India, where people worship over 22 million gods and even pray to McDonald's toys from the 1990s for good health, wealth, abundance, and prosperity. Yet when they hear the message of Jesus, witness His power through miracles, and feel a profound presence that surpasses the many gods and temples they have known, they discover a completely new life filled with purpose and meaning! People who would never die for their gods or beliefs are now willing to bridge the gap between heaven and darkness. Hindu and Muslim Extremists threaten their very existence, subjecting them to severe violence for their faith in Jesus. What grants them such strength if Jesus is not real?

I think of Stephen in Acts 7:55, where he was being stoned to death because he believed in Jesus. Acts says, "But he, being full of the Holy Spirit, looked up steadfastly into heaven, and saw the glory of God, and Jesus standing on the right hand of God, and said, Behold, I see the heavens opened, and the Son of man standing on the right hand of God." This incredible power enables individuals to see a greater purpose and vision, even in the face of death. The very one who ordered Stephen's stoning was Paul, who experienced an extraordinary encounter with Jesus himself. After this transformative experience, Paul dedicated his life to serving Jesus, enduring persecution, rejection, and mockery from others. He even relinquished his high authority and status in Jerusalem to embrace this newfound life.

I also think about these words of Jesus, "Behold, I have given you authority to tread upon serpents and scorpions, and over all the power of the enemy: and nothing shall in any wise hurt you." Does this mean nothing will ever harm you? Of course not. He is saying that you will have power over the forces of darkness and the flesh that exists in this world, even unto death, as Revelation 2:10 mentions.

In my travels and preaching about Jesus, I faced life-threatening situations numerous times. However, it wasn't my time; for Stephen, it was his time as he witnessed the glory of God. I have had guns pointed at me, guns fired at me and faced threats with knives and other weapons. I have witnessed the power of God manifest in ways that caused people to drop to the ground, unable to lift their hands to attack.

One time, a man charged at me, cursing and screaming, yet what appeared to be a massive spirit, the size of a six-story building, intervened between us. He seemed to hit an invisible wall, fell completely on his back, and appeared stunned, confused, and silent. After a moment, he stood up and turned in the opposite direction as if nothing had happened while I continued to preach the gospel of Jesus.

I also recall meeting an elderly woman who heard me street preach in Times Square, New York City. She encouraged me not to stop and said, "God will do incredible things in your life." I asked her if she personally knew David Wilkerson, the former pastor of Times Square Church, before his death. She replied, "Yes, I did." She had participated in prayer groups with him and urged me, saying, "never stop because the spirit of God is alive in you. You will see even greater things than this."

The words of Jesus came to life for me. "Heal the sick, raise the dead, cleanse the lepers, cast out demons: freely you received, freely give." I have experienced this firsthand by praying for a woman with elephantiasis, resulting in her giant leg being healed. I have seen individuals suffering from severe back pain and spine issues who could hardly walk, find instant healing. I've witnessed miracles where people with cancer and seizure disorders were healed instantly. I prayed for healing over someone with a crippled hand and a painful throat, unable to sing or play the guitar, and they were immediately healed. This person returned to their doctor, and imaging confirmed complete healing in both areas. I have seen people with drug and alcohol addictions delivered instantaneously. Those with same-sex desires and tendencies have found freedom from their chains, and individuals struggling with pornography and sexual addictions have been set free. How could this be? Some may say, "Why don't I see this today? How do I know it's real?"

I am reminded of Jesus's words in Matthew 13:58 "And he did not many mighty works there because of their unbelief." It was his hometown and region. I have encountered situations where people with great faith and those with little faith were not healed; however, some of them did experience healing. In countries outside of America, I witnessed greater miracles and a deeper move of the Holy Spirit. Jesus says, "Blessed are they that hunger and thirst after righteousness: for they shall be filled." There's a reason God moves in some places more than others, depending on their heart's desire to be delivered, set free, and live for him.

I remember praying for a homeless man who, upon handing him a tract about the gospel and God's salvation and love, read and stared down at it for over 10 minutes. I sat down and talked with him. I discovered that he was raped by his uncle and molested and raped by his foster parent. He drank alcohol to numb the pain, but he was dying and tormented inside. I prayed for his deliverance from demons, placing my hand on his upper back. Suddenly, I felt a pop, and he slumped down in tears. As time passed, he looked up with a new glow, a fiery light in his eyes, and a joy so strong that not even the darkest depression could fill any crevice within him. Didn't the same situation occur with Jesus, who delivered a violent and angry man from demons in Matthew 8:28-34?

For some, this may be a concept they have never heard of before. Practices such as meditation, yoga, chakra alignment, energy healing, reiki, tantras, fortune telling, horoscopes, astrology, and various religions can open individuals up to the risk of demonic possession or the influence of familiar spirits that are not aligned with the one true Holy Spirit.

I saw a woman drop a piece of paper while walking out of a building. I bent down to pick it up and handed it to her. She glanced at me briefly but then quickly turned her gaze away, appearing very anxious. I noticed a sense of darkness and pain in her eyes. As I walked around the corner of the street, it struck me that she had just come out of a tarot card reading. I've encountered many experiences like this, such as a woman who was physically and sexually abused as a child and grew up in a broken home. She identified as a Satanist and feminist and struggled with deep anger toward her father due to her abusive upbringing. Her husband listened to my sermons, which touched on new-age practices, and he was delivered. Meanwhile, his wife was resistant and filled with anger, even wishing for my death. She harbored hatred toward me and resented her husband.

One day, she heard my message and broke down in tears. She smashed her crystals and prayer grid, burned her tarot cards, and destroyed every witchcraft book and material she owned. This act marked the beginning of a new life for her. She radiated a new spirit, and her eyes sparkled with love and joy. This transformation reminds me of Acts 19:19, "And a number of those who practiced magical arts brought their books together and burned them in the sight of all; and they counted the price of them, and found it fifty thousand pieces of silver" (several million US dollars). Imagine discovering a power greater than anything on earth!

I have discovered that those seeking fulfillment outside of God often turn to practices such as witchcraft, Ouija boards, tarot cards, fortune telling, magic, spell jars, crystal grids, horoscopes, and fortune tellers. This desire usually stems from a need to take control of their lives and futures, often fueled by anger toward those who have hurt them. They seek ways to ensure that no one has the power to hurt them again. Oftentimes, there is spiritual, physical, religious, or sexual abuse. In their rage, they will often turn to dark spirits and practices to regain a sense of control and order in their lives. They may feel a sense of power but need constant spiritual experiences to find peace, but they will never experience rest. These practices teach us to have power over hate, but God gives us rest with forgiveness and give up the sense of control. The very thing that they desire in life is the truth that one often wrestles against. Life is unpredictable, and the world can change in an instant.

However, there is one who maintains control, even when we feel powerless.

God is real, Jesus is real, and there is a greater purpose to life that many are beginning to discover! Among all the religions, lifestyles, and spiritual experiences in this world, there is only one true source of freedom, healing, and peace that surpasses all human understanding and the complexities of our existence.

"People who would never die for their gods or beliefs are now willing to bridge the gap between heaven and darkness. Hindu and Muslim Extremists threaten their very existence, subjecting them to severe violence for their faith in Jesus. What grants them such strength if Jesus is not real?"

-*Todd Aaron*

Chapter 8: A New Life

Hebrews 2:14-15 states, "Since then the children are sharers in flesh and blood, he also himself in like manner partook of the same; that through death he might destroy him that had the power of death, that is, the devil; and might deliver all them who through fear of death were all their lifetime subject to bondage." In Galatians 5:16 it says, "But I say, walk by the Spirit, and ye shall not fulfill the lust of the flesh." Romans 6:14 says, "For sin shall not have dominion over you: for ye are not under law, but under grace."

What is the grace of God given by the Holy Spirit to those who repent from their sins and desire to be saved? Titus 2:11-14 "For the grace of God has appeared, bringing salvation to all men, instructing us, to the intent that, denying ungodliness and worldly lusts, we should live soberly and righteously and godly in this present world; looking for the blessed hope and appearing of the glory of the great God and our Savior Jesus Christ; who gave himself for us, that he might redeem us from all iniquity, and purify unto himself a people for his own possession, zealous of good works."

This goal is the purpose of life: to be freed from death unto life! We must transform our character into His character, and our morals and values should align with His. Our aim for desires and longings to resemble His as well. John 15:26-27 "But when the Comforter is come, whom I will send unto you from the Father, *even* the Spirit of truth, which proceeds from the Father, he shall bear witness of me: and you also bear witness, because you have been with me from the beginning." What was from the beginning? The Word and the Spirit. He gave both of these to all who believed in and desired to discover this newfound life and purpose. You will know right and wrong, understand guilt and shame, and know how to live with peace, love, and joy. Peace is what God promises to all who walk with him. John 14:27 "Peace I leave with you; my peace I give unto you: not as the world giveth, give I unto you. Let not your heart be troubled, neither let it be fearful."

The law always proceeds before the gospel so that we recognize our sins and can become convicted of those sins. It's the only discovery on this Earth that convicts people of wrongdoing yet offers true freedom and healing. How is it that one such as myself and those in prison can forgive those in their past that hurt them? And how is it possible to hold a heart full of love and forgiveness? Can any human experience on Earth lead to such a profound understanding? Certainly, anyone can be kind and perform nice acts for others. During the pandemic, I witnessed a man—broken, hurt, suffering from alcohol addiction, and a history of rape and molestation—who managed to forgive and find healing. A woman wearing a double facemask, face shield, hazmat suit, and gloves and, using a trash picker, handed this man food in a styrofoam container.

Others, including myself, sat with him out of compassion and love, without fear of sickness. This woman, dressed in all her protection, was part of an organization combining New Age beliefs with Buddhist and Hindu practices.

Psalms 95:3 "For the Lord is the great God, the great King above all gods." 1 John 4:8 "Whoever does not love does not know God, because God is love."

In today's modern age, we often hear phrases like "love is love" and "all you need is love." However, these sentiments often reflect humanism and a human understanding of love. But what actually constitutes compassion and love? Anyone can give money, donate clothes, volunteer at homeless shelters, feed those experiencing poverty, and do kind things for others. Is this really the kind of love that surpasses human understanding? Ephesians 3:19 says, "May you experience the love of Christ, though it is too great to understand fully. Then you will be made complete with all the fullness of life and power that comes from God."

When I witnessed the tragic death of a woman in a car accident while her husband and their three-year-old child survived, I was overwhelmed with deep sadness and compassion. Meanwhile, people around the scene took pictures and videos, including news crews. I found myself praying for the family, deeply moved and saddened. This child would have to grow up without a mother, and the husband would face life without his wife. While others may have felt sorrow, few seemed to engage in genuine empathy; instead, their attention was on their phones.

How is it that clinics claiming to care for women offer free abortions, yet adoption can cost $30,000 to $40,000 in the U.S.? Some women's clinics provide not just resources but also financial and physical assistance, counseling, the love of Jesus, compassionate care, and free checkups and ultrasounds. Many people can perform acts of kindness, but how many genuinely exhibit deep, compassionate care for another person's heart, soul, and mind? How many genuinely love their neighbor as themselves? Who is truly invested in seeing change and healing in others rather than treating patients like mere subjects in a medical system that quickly prescribes drugs and says, "You'll have a checkup in a few weeks?" Who sincerely wants others to discover healing and love because of the love God has shown you? Some may yet find that they love themselves, and my heart goes out to you. Many may still carry questions, hurt, pain, anger, and hatred. Yet, I have witnessed how a desperate cry for salvation can lead to freedom through Jesus.

Consider Jesus, who approached those afflicted with leprosy—a disease so severe that its victims were quarantined outside the walls of Jerusalem. Many of these individuals lived for decades without ever experiencing touch, a hug, a kiss, or any expression of compassion. Picture Jesus walking toward them in a hazmat suit, delivering food with a trash picker! Instead, He approached them directly, touched them, and healed them. Similarly, Jesus healed a man paralyzed for 38 years at the Pool of Bethesda. While people rushed to the waters believing they possessed healing properties, this paralyzed man had no one to assist him because everyone was focused solely on themselves. But Jesus, filled with compassion, recognized the man's heart and faith and healed him. I imagine people walked up to him and fed him, but when it came to true healing, no one had the love of God filled with compassion to sit down with him to heal this suffering soul.

Many come to Jesus seeking something tangible, just as the 5,000 gathered to hear Him speak, attracted by the promise of physical nourishment. I have seen this in various countries where people listen to the message but are primarily interested in the food offered. Jesus pointed out this behavior in John 6:26-27, saying, "Jesus answered them and said, Verily, verily, I say unto you, You seek me, not because you saw signs, but because you ate of the loaves, and were filled. Work not for the food which perishes, but for the food which abides unto eternal life, which the Son of man shall give unto you: for him the Father, *even* God, has sealed." The true bread of life and living water.

John 6:36 "Then Jesus declared, "I am the bread of life. Whoever comes to me will never go hungry, and whoever believes in me will never be thirsty." This concept can be difficult for some to grasp. Just as people in Jesus' time were concerned about money, health, food, and drink, the same is true today. However, what is the true meaning of life and purpose?

I remember when food was my idol, although I didn't realize it then. It wasn't until I became sick with Lyme disease and was later diagnosed with celiac disease and several food sensitivities that I began to see things differently. As a result of these challenges, I recognized that the true "bread of life" and "living water" are far more valuable than simply eating and drinking. I recall going to restaurants where people felt bad because I couldn't eat. My gums would swell, and I suffered from severe gut issues, diarrhea, nausea, headaches, liver pain, and an overall feeling of being unwell. Through this, I learned that the social aspects of dining out, eating at friends' homes, hosting guests, and enjoying food and drink were no longer fulfilling for me. Ultimately, I discovered a greater purpose: life is more than just eating and drinking. Solomon, the richest man to have ever lived, said, "There is nothing better for a man *than* that he should eat and drink, and make his soul enjoy good in his labor. This also I saw that it is from the hand of God." Yet, I found that the greatest joy known to humanity was stripped away due to my unrecognized desire for more. I learned a deeper purpose in life when he said, "Fear God and keep His commandments; for this is the whole duty of man."

Romans 14:17 also reminds us, "For the kingdom of God is not a matter of eating and drinking but of righteousness and peace and joy in the Holy Spirit." Through my suffering, I learned the language of compassion, which communicates more profoundly than the 7,139 known languages of humanity. As Hebrews 5:8 states, Jesus learned obedience through suffering. We do not come to Jesus to escape sickness, eliminate poverty, end death, or solve financial troubles, but rather to be freed from sin, healed from within, and to find peace that surpasses human understanding. We are called to love our neighbors as we love ourselves and cherish His commandments, which teach us how to live and treat one another. Solomon also said in Ecclesiastes 8:17 "Then I saw all that God has done. No one can comprehend what goes on under the sun. Despite all their efforts to search it out, no one can discover its meaning. Even if the wise claim they know, they cannot really comprehend it." Many search for meaning and purpose yet never truly grasp it, even when they claim to know it. Even those who believe they understand the purpose of life or their purpose often fail to truly discover it.

"The purpose of life: to be freed from death unto life! We must transform our character into His character, and our morals and values should align with His." *-Todd Aaron*

Chapter 9: What Has One Missed?

A wealthy man in the Bible placed Jesus in his costly tomb. Again, a rich woman anointed Jesus' feet with perfume before his crucifixion. While Jesus was pinned to the cross, he would have had to exert strength to lift his feet and wrists to gasp for air. With each breath, he would have caught the sweet, soothing aroma of the perfume. Jesus remarked that the memory of this woman's act would always be spoken of from that point onward.

Next to Jesus on the cross, one man mocked and derided him. He was stubborn, prideful, arrogant, and haughty. The man to the other side of him, also nailed to a cross, admitted his sins and wrongdoings, and asked Jesus for forgiveness, recognizing Jesus' true identity. Jesus responded, "Today, you will be with me in paradise." This second man was humble, repentant, remorseful, contrite in spirit and heart, and desperate for salvation.

Some rich and poor alike know they need a savior, such as the many prostitutes, murderers, and drunkards that I've encountered. They understand what they have been delivered from and what God continues to save them from. At the same time, others scoff at God or the name of Jesus, who hear and become angry at anything related to the Bible. Who do you think will receive healing, freedom, and salvation?

I went to a prison in Guatemala where I was about to preach. The sorrow and pain from God were so intense that I felt it weighing heavily on my heart and soul. Deep within those concrete walls and iron bars, I was overwhelmed by the love God has for these souls, who are not only imprisoned within themselves but also physically separated from the outside world. I watched some people around me conversing, eating, and drinking, yet I couldn't join them. My heart was burdened with anguish. God's words began to overflow from within me with no prior plans for a message—except for what He gave me in just 10 minutes. As I spoke, I felt an incredible power surging through me, so much so that I thought an earthquake might happen. The Spirit was flowing abundantly in that prison. After I finished speaking, men throughout the room began to rise from their seats, tears streaming down their faces as they prostrated themselves on the cold concrete floor. I joined them on the ground, crying out for their salvation. Many people were kneeling in front of their seats, weeping in anguish. More than 200 individuals in the prison were in tears. This moment was not just a spiritual experience bursting with emotions; it was a sincere struggle against the flesh for deliverance by the Holy Spirit and salvation through the grace of Jesus. I hugged many people, shook hands, and reassured them of God's great love for them. In that prison, I shared with them what God had revealed to me, "You are blessed, whether you recognize it or not. Many outside these walls are too distracted by the things of this life, but you have more time to pray and draw near to God than most people in the world."

I have preached to gangs and violent individuals in the streets, prisons, and churches of all sizes. If it's one thing I have discovered, God is patient and loves people deeply. Do you want to find a greater purpose? 2 Peter 3:9 says, "The Lord is not slack concerning his promise, as some count slackness; but is longsuffering, not wishing that any should perish, but that all should come to repentance." Jesus said, "For I was hungry, and you gave Me something to eat; I was thirsty, and you gave Me something to drink; I was a stranger, and you invited Me in; naked, and you clothed Me; I was sick, and you visited Me; I was in prison, and you came to Me." What do we see here? A deep, unending compassion and love beyond human ability.

Before I found Jesus, I thought I was loving and kind. Perhaps I was, but I didn't truly understand the depth of love at that time. My love wasn't like a deep well overflowing with living water. Whenever I traveled to other countries to do God's work, I was passionate about sharing the message of God's love and saving grace, helping others understand His word. I would return to America in tears, crying at the airport, on the plane, in the bathroom, in the shower, driving, and even at home. Why? Because so many in America are distracted, walking with their noses in the air, lacking love and care. They are lost, broken, and stubborn. You see a stubborn pride that shows little concern for others and what truly matters in life. When you try to strike up a conversation about the gospel, share what God has done for you, or even discuss sins, people often smirk, roll their eyes, and give you a strange look. The same observances can be seen in Western Europe, the United Kingdom, Australia, and many wealthier countries.

It reminds me of the community in ancient times in Revelation 3:17, which says, "Because you say, 'I am rich; I have acquired wealth and do not need a thing.' But you do not realize that you are wretched, pitiful, poor, blind, and naked." I see this growing by the multitudes. If you visit most churches in these first-world countries, they often do not feel compelled to take any action outside of their own congregations. It's similar to a sports team that only reads, studies, practices, and plays within its arena but never competes against other teams.

Matthew 3:11 says, "He shall baptize you in the Holy Spirit and *in* fire." If the Holy Spirit truly transforms a person rather than just causing a moment of emotionalism, wouldn't you feel a burning zeal and a fire that consumes the flesh to invigorate the spirit within? If you see people boarding a plane that appears unsafe, with loose turbines that you know haven't been properly inspected, would you remain silent and allow them to board, knowing it could crash and result in fatalities? If you were on that plane, someone entered and said, "Get off this plane! I care about your life. This plane is going to crash!" Would you choose to ignore the warning, or would you feel compelled to warn others as well, wanting to save them just as you were saved? In the same way, how could one receive salvation and still ignore the dangers lurking around in the lives of others?

You can never do the work of God with a spirit of pride, ego, or a desire for power and control. Your motives must be pure, driven by sincere concern, love, and care for others—qualities that stem from the love Jesus poured into your life. Jesus says, "Those who have ears, let them hear." Don't waste your time trying to save or help those who refuse the help. Instead, go to those with open hearts. Those whom God leads you to, and who He says, "That one." God knows the hearts and minds of everyone. As Matthew 18:12 says, "If a man has a hundred sheep, and one of them has gone astray, does he not leave the ninety-nine on the mountains and go in search of the one that gone astray?" Without a shepherd, sheep may walk off a cliff or be devoured by wolves. We will go astray in the world without His lead.

Jesus says in John 10:27-28 "My sheep hear my voice, and I know them, and they follow me. And I give unto them eternal life; and they shall never perish, neither shall any man pluck them out of my hand." What greater joy is there than to find inner freedom and have a purpose in the world that exceeds human comprehension? Jesus says in Matthew

16:25 "For whoever wants to save their life will lose it, but whoever loses their life for me will find it."

I have observed that those who falsely come to Jesus or who express hatred towards Him often still cling to and love their lives. They may not realize how empty and dead they feel inside, which drives them to seek external needs and desires to fill a broken and painful soul. Many love the things of the world so intensely that their desire to preserve their lives prevents them from achieving the true healing that would lead them to freedom. Jesus, through His Spirit, promises to remove the stony heart—one that is angry, bitter, rebellious, and resentful toward God. He will cleanse it from the love for sin and its enticing desires.

Many people in first-world countries desire to be pampered, have a sense of entitlement, seek to be served, and receive preferential treatment. It's common in countries like America, Canada, and Western Europe. They quickly become angry when their food or drink orders aren't perfect, when service isn't immediate, or when they don't receive the pampering they expect at hotels or resorts. This observation highlights that many individuals have a superficial lifestyle and attitude.

I witnessed an American in Costa Rica trying to appear wealthy, speaking arrogantly and treating the waiter as if they were beneath them. This individual complained about an additional $1.00 drink charge on their receipt and created a scene, treating the waitress poorly. I've often observed them snapping their fingers, not saying please and thank you, or being kind. I have observed loud and haughty laughs and discussions from Americans in most countries. Sadly, this attitude, derived from pride, grew within Babylon and was comparable to America and first-world countries, including the haughtiness of Switzerland, Australia, and some other NATO countries.

As Ezekiel 16:50 says, "And they were haughty and committed abomination before Me; therefore, I took them away as I saw fit." Haughty means proud, arrogant, lordly, insolent, overbearing, supercilious, and disdainful, showing scorn for inferiors and those under them and having a sense of superiority. Isn't this what we see in the hearts of many who have lost purpose in life and reject Jesus? Sadly, some of these have poorly represented the holy name of Jesus and even abused others in the name of Jesus. Instead of being a light to the world, they walk around in darkness and use the Bible as if to carry cattle prodding iron, burning and hurting individuals. As Matthew 7:14 says, "But small is the gate and narrow the road that leads to life, and only a few find it." Indeed, this verse speaks more volumes than all the books in the world. Who will honestly find purpose and meaning in their life?

"We've reduced God to a minimum. Most of us are trying to get to heaven with minimum spirituality. If we looked after our business like we look after our soul, we'd be bankrupt years ago! The materialism has crept in and it's blinded us! It (has become) a way of life." -*Leonard Ravenhill*

Chapter 10: Discovering Greater Purpose

Imagine for a moment someone approached you and said, "I want to give you a mansion, a car, and ten million dollars." How would you respond? How grateful would you feel to receive a gift like this? What if they extended the offer by saying, "I also want to give you a private tropical island." How much more thankful and enthusiastic would you be to tell everyone about what this person has offered you?

But then they continue, "There are a few rules to accepting it. No parties, no drugs, no getting drunk, no pornography, no sex outside of marriage, worship Jesus, don't steal, don't lie, and love your neighbor as yourself." Could you follow these rules?

That's what salvation is with Jesus. Salvation through Jesus brings profound peace, surpassing worldly possessions and offering rest from fleshly desires. We find this in Matthew 13:44-46. "The kingdom of heaven is like unto a treasure hidden in the field; which a man found and hid; and in his joy he goes and sells all that he has, and buys that field. Again, the kingdom of heaven is like unto a man that is a merchant seeking goodly pearls: and having found one pearl of great price, he went and sold all that he had and bought it." Do you see it? What is the value of eternal life and finding your purpose in life? Isn't it so priceless that no money or possessions could ever buy? Purpose can never be bought, but it can be found.

I heard a song a while back by George Strait called "The Little Things." He's speaking about life going by so fast that you miss the little things. He begins to describe the little things he discovered that hold value. He mentions how everyone seeks the meaning and secrets to life, yet the more one searches, the more one realizes it's right there, hiding in plain sight. He begins to mention the little things that have purpose and not to let the big things get in the way of the little things. These words are valid.

With each child I have, I learn more and become more patient. As the years passed, I realized how much I had previously missed. The closer I draw to God through prayer and reading His word, the more I discover, love, and feel humbled. I have learned to appreciate the simple joys in life—watching trees sway, birds fly, holding my little girl, walking barefoot in nature, singing songs to God, holding hands with my wife during a stroll, sitting on a swing, and taking in the sunset. I find joy in gazing at the stars at night, enjoying calm drives with the windows down while feeling the warm breeze, watching ocean waves, taking photos with strangers for a laugh, lying in a hammock, riding in the back of a truck, soaking up the sun's rays, admiring the beauty of flowers, and watching animals roam and play. I also enjoy going out of my way to help older adults I see struggling when I'm out and about. I recognize they are someone's mother, father, grandparent, or beloved elder. I strive to brighten someone's day in any way I can—not out of religious obligation, a desire for recognition, or legalism, but from pure joy, love, and care for others. This attitude is not something I could have developed on my own; it is a transformation that God has brought about in my life.

People consistently tell me, "You're so kind, respectful, and well-mannered." In a world where hearts and love seem to be growing cold, it's important to maintain your love for God. Naturally, this love will reflect how you treat others. Throughout my life journey, I set out to discover my purpose. There came a moment when I needed to silence everything and escape the noise surrounding me. I realized that although I was alive, I wasn't truly living. I did nice things for people, knew Jesus, had a wife and kids, and shared the message of Jesus with others. I even gave away so much money that I could have bought a house. However, I had to find my purpose alone. I needed to connect with myself and spend time with God. This meant exploring the world, searching deep within, and reflecting on my past, present, and future.

I remember boarding a plane to a place I had never been, overwhelmed and burdened, unsure of who I was or why I was there. My wife sensed my struggle and encouraged me to do whatever I needed to find clarity. I began exploring and adventuring without an agenda, timeframe, expectations, concern about finances, or when my journey would end. Time for me didn't exist, as I woke up and took things slow, sipping coffee for three hours. I explored different regions, sometimes sitting and staring at nature or conversing with random people. What was I looking for? Who is this person? What am I looking for? I had everything society deemed valuable and even possessed things many believers in Jesus would only dream of. Yet, there I was, searching, questioning, wondering, observing, and trying to discover more about myself.

I came to the realization that despite all the good things I have done for others, my family, and God, I have yet to find myself or take the time to truly understand who I am. I was moving through life without grasping my purpose. Like many others, I held misconceptions about what purpose really means. How could someone who healed the sick, delivered people from demons, and brought many to find peace, love, joy, and freedom suddenly find themselves in a place of uncertainty about their own identity? Some believed I was suicidal, but few understood my true condition. I realized God guided me on a deeper path of letting go of my flesh. Like gold refined by fire, I needed to be tested for purity, allowing the impurities to be removed. Those substances that do not belong in a pure and holy place must be stripped away. As Jesus said, "You are the temple of God," and that temple houses the Holy Spirit, just as it did in ancient times.

As a lamb was being strapped down and prepped to be sacrificed, you would see your reflection in the brass of the altar as the flesh burned off the animal that never deserved death. I felt I could see my own reflection in Jesus on the cross as if I were kneeling before him. Like the sacrificial lamb, the flesh that rules over you must be burned off. After the refining and burning of our flesh on the brazen altar, we will then have a pleasing aroma burning like incense from the golden altar, which burns day and night. At this point in my life, Jesus was inviting me to view the world through the eyes of the cross, as if I were in the process of becoming crucified alongside Him. This extreme revelation and heartfelt longing stirred deep within my soul and being.

I started seeing the souls in people rather than their physical forms. I began to perceive my own soul more and my flesh less. We must find our purpose in life, not only in the world but in eternity. Have you had a revelation of eternity? Or is it merely another glimpse of an earthly purpose? Those who are aware that they are dying, often find true life.

At the same time, those who are oblivious to their impending mortality have yet to discover what it means to truly live.

Each person must bear their cross and undergo a kind of crucifixion. If you believe you are living solely in the flesh, you must undergo this crucifixion again. A prideful or stubborn person stabs the side of Jesus and gambles for His clothes, while a humble and surrendered person weeps like Jesus' mother. They show sincere care for others, like the disciple who looked after Jesus' mother as if she were his own.

A soul dying from their flesh can see the hearts of others and becomes filled with compassion and sadness. The one who loves deeply has been forgiven deeply. When someone stops loving and becomes devoid of compassion, they lose sight of their former condition and form themselves into a god. The God I know died so that everyone, including you, might have eternal life! Lazarus was raised from the dead and walked out of the tomb. A dead man heard the voice of God and rose from the dead into life. If the dead can hear God's voice, why aren't many of the living listening? It's because the living fail to hear God's call or recognize that they are dying!

Those who die will surely live again, and the Spirit will raise them up in the last days or at the grave. I think of my wife's grandmother, whose mother hid in Nazi Germany during the Holocaust, secretly observing God's Jewish holy days. She was a woman of God who, years ago, urgently handed me a Bible while shaking, telling me how vital it was for her to give it to me because God wanted her to. She fervently prayed for the husband that my wife would marry.

When my wife's grandmother passed away, I learned that she had led a significant women's ministry, adopted a child, raised her children, cared for her husband, and dedicated herself to incredible acts of love for people and God's kingdom. Many people expressed their gratitude for her loving kindness and said she taught them the words of God alongside her husband. I realized she lived with a clear purpose and discovered the meaning of life.

I lost both of my grandmothers in the same year long ago, but for some reason, my wife's grandmother's passing affected me differently. Could it be that God was revealing a deeper understanding and perspective on life as I matured and embarked on this journey? I thought about Proverbs 22:1: "A good name is more desirable than great riches; to be esteemed is better than silver or gold." It's better to be known for what you have done for God and others than for any other purpose in life.

The value of eternity far outweighs any price that man can place upon anything on this earth. The ones with the bad reputation are the ones forgotten. Those with a tarnished reputation are forgotten over time. A celebrity may be remembered for their acting or music, but that remembrance is different from the lasting legacy of someone who has lived for God. Eventually, people might acknowledge those celebrities through documentaries or books, but as generations pass, their value and contributions may fade from memory. Anyone existing hardly pays attention to what their great-grandparents, or even their great, great, great grandparents, have done.

What truly matters? Living for God, allowing your actions to reflect His character, sharing His love, and raising your children to do the same. I ponder how God's design works and how generations and life led up to the moment my wife and I met, married, and had children. Imagine if my wife's grandmother had not lived according to God's purpose for her life—how differently would our future have looked? Every decision you make in life affects not only you and others but also future generations. One person's lifestyle and decisions can impact the entire world.

Let your purpose and existence be a gift to others and God.

Chapter 11: What Is My Purpose?

Everyone is searching for purpose and the mystery behind it. Many still wonder what their true purpose is in life. We find ourselves at a crossroads, faced with two paths: one that leads to death and one to life. The Bible can be seen as an acronym for "Basic Instructions Before Leaving Earth." However, very few people treasure it or truly understand the manual for building a purpose-driven life. Many are hesitant to stand apart and go against the currents of this world. Like David confronting Goliath, we must face our inner giants and overcome temptations that come against our hearts and minds. Achieving this requires submitting to a higher purpose to maintain the peace that comes from God. Jesus says in John 14:27, "Peace I leave with you; my peace I give to you: I do not give to you as the world gives. Let not your heart be troubled, neither let it be fearful."

True purpose is not about leaving this world or having nothing; it is about resisting the influences that may pull us away from God or cause us to harbor hatred toward others, which robs us of compassion. Compassion is defined as the act of showing or having mercy, sympathy, empathy, or pity. The Bible translates it as "womb" or "deeply moved." Just as a mother is deeply moved by the child she carries; we should extend that same sense of compassion to others in their various circumstances.

It's challenging for people to fully embody the words of Romans 12:15, "Rejoice with those who rejoice; mourn with those who mourn." Similarly, 1 Corinthians 12:26 states, "If one member suffers, all suffer together; if one member is honored, all rejoice together." Psalm 133:1 beautifully expresses, "How good and pleasant it is when God's people live together in unity!" God has a plan, a purpose, and a life for each of us. I remember two individuals I was close to, one of whom I held in high regard for the help he provided me. We went hiking up a mountain so high in elevation that one developed a massive headache and couldn't catch his breath. The other man continued without looking back, even ignoring my concern, when I yelled to him, "Hey, he's struggling here." I sat down to support the one in difficulty while the other man kept walking his way up.

Halfway up, I decided to stop for the one who was struggling. The man who continued up the mountain had blood coming from his nose, a severe headache, felt dizzy, and experienced intense ear pain. Nevertheless, he prayed to God for the endurance to finish this race in life. It wasn't until later I realized the deeper meaning of that day. The man who stopped eventually took a different path and chose a different spiritual journey, which I still pray for to this day. Through many trials,

I understood that God was telling me, "Keep going. Don't look back, don't let anyone distract you, and don't worry about their walk, or else it will slow down the purpose and plans that I have for you."

One must inherit tunnel vision for the kingdom and his purpose. 2 Timothy 2:4 says, "No soldier on service entangles himself in the affairs of *this* life; that he may please him who enrolled him as a soldier." Remember, your goal is to please God, not man. Too many people become consumed by worldly affairs, worries, and distractions.

Recently, I delivered a sermon at a humble church where I spoke on several important topics. For instance, 1 John 2:17, "And the world passes away, and the lust thereof: but he that does the will of God abides for ever." I mentioned James 4:14, which says, "What is your life? For you are a vapor that appears for a little time, and then vanishes away." I also discussed the parable of the four seeds in Matthew chapter thirteen. In this parable, the seeds represent the word of God, the soil symbolizes people's hearts, the birds signify the devil, and the rocks represent temptations. The thorns reflect the worries, riches, and pleasures of this life, while the fruit represents obedience, good works, and faithfulness. I emphasized that being faithful to God is like being faithful to a spouse in marriage. The good works are not to obtain salvation but are the fruit and evidence of our salvation through God's grace and the Holy Spirit. I began to say, "How you may have heard the Word, but where are your hearts?"

Some may hear the word of God, represented by the seeds, but the devil steals them away. The devil swiftly steals the Word that would take root. Others may hear God's word, but those seeds fall on rocky ground due to life's temptations and sins, failing to take root and bear fruit. The words never took root to bear good fruits as evidence of the Spirit. Galatians 5:22-23 describes the fruits of the Spirit as "love, joy, peace, patience, kindness, goodness, faithfulness, gentleness, and self-control." Self-control is the power over sin, which God says His Spirit empowers us to overcome.

As we continue with the seeds, some are choked out by thorns, preventing the Son of God from reaching them with his light and nurturing them to grow. This causes individuals to become ensnared by the worries of wealth, materialism, and the pleasures of life, leading to a lack of spiritual fruitfulness.

I also discussed the parable of the great banquet and wedding feast in Luke 14. This illustrates those invited to God's kingdom and called to live like Jesus while bearing fruit, yet many make excuses not to attend. One person says, "I just bought a field; I must go see it. Please excuse me." This reflects someone preoccupied with property, house, or land, neglecting the deeper aspects of God and His kingdom. Another said, "I just bought five yoke of oxen; I'm on my way to try them out. Please excuse me." This shows a heart focused on work, career, or business rather than the significant matters of God and His kingdom. Another claims, "I just got married, so I cannot come." This person was consumed by the responsibilities of marriage and tending to his wife and, maybe, his kids, losing sight of the value of God and His kingdom.

There's meaning behind Jesus instructing us to go into the streets and alleys to bring in the poor, crippled, blind, and lame, emphasizing that there is still room for more. These people are souls reached with the gospel of Jesus and presented with the word of God with all wisdom, knowledge, and understanding of the seed of life presented to them. Yet, it is ultimately their choice between life and death, to seek the precious pearl and the treasure hidden in the field.

To discover the greatest value in Jesus and His kingdom, one must treasure it in their heart and live for Him. Jesus said that those originally invited would not taste his banquet. Jesus warns that those originally invited will not taste His banquet. These are often individuals found in the church, believed to be saved, engaged in religious practices, and having heard God's Word from an early age. They are preoccupied with the affairs of this life and miss the opportunity to bear fruit and truly appreciate the gift of grace from God. This gift of grace, His Word, and the Spirit that existed from the beginning illuminate a dark world, yearning for a future free from pain, suffering, and sorrow, as all former things will pass away. Revelation 22:17 states, "And the Spirit and the bride say, Come. And he that hears, let him say, Come. And he that is thirsty, let him come: he that will, let him take the water of life freely." This is a freely given gift; the more one partakes of the living water, the more one will discover their purpose.

The more one has eyes for eternity; the more one will come to know God's plans for their life. Pray for wisdom, discernment, knowledge, understanding, and prophecy. Pray that God will use you to connect with others so they may know His love for them. Pray that God's will is done on earth as it is in heaven. Remember to pray for others, especially those who come to mind. Pray for others and whoever comes to mind during prayer. Pray to see through the eyes that He sees through and see the world the way that He does. When you pray all of these words with full sincerity and from a pure heart, don't expect ever to see life the same again. Don't be surprised when you're burdened, filled with anguish, sorrow, and yet great joy. You will begin to see people's souls as Jesus sees them rather than their flesh as humans see them. The more that you love Jesus and realize how much he loves you, the greater you will love others and care deeply for them and their soul. You can read the Bible and learn the teaching and instructions in Proverbs, but if your heart is not set on doing the will of God, then that knowledge remains unfulfilled—lacking understanding and the application of wisdom.

If a vessel becomes filled with mud or another liquid, how can God fill it with pure, living water? To be filled, you must first become emptied. Furthermore, living water is constantly moving and flowing; if the water sits too long, it will grow bacteria of mildew. You must keep pouring out into others to be filled more. John 7:38 says, "He that believes on me, as the scripture hath said, from within him shall flow rivers of living water." The greater the measure of one's faith, the more he will pour into you. Many people do not receive this because they lack the faith to act on God's movement through the Holy Spirit. Some may fear that they won't do it right or won't hear God's voice correctly.

However, the more you walk by faith and not by sight, the more your faith will grow. Jesus tells us that faith as small as a mustard seed can move mountains—mountains that represent kingdoms, nations, and many people. Truly, God can perform miraculous works through a humble vessel that is emptied of itself and willing to be filled with the holy waters gifted from above.

Romans 15:13, "Now the God of hope fill you with all joy and peace in believing, that you may abound in hope, in the power of the Holy Spirit." As you strive to hear the words, "Well done my good and faithful servant," as you enter the joy and kingdom of God with rest for eternity, it's important to discover your purpose in life and live for it right now. Serve with passion, love with passion, give with passion, speak and preach with passion, and live and breathe with passion for Jesus and God's kingdom. Love God's commandments with passion, and love others as yourself with passion.

Man and woman of God, never engage in the work of God until you discover fervent zeal and passion. Only then will you be useful for God's kingdom without the flesh hindering the work of the Holy Spirit by you operating in the flesh. What do you think being baptized with spirit and fire truly means? Discover how great God's love is, and you will uncover your purpose. Romans 8:28 says, "And we know that to them that love God all things work together for good, *even* to them that are called according to *his* purpose." Amen.

Chapter 12: Remaining In Purpose with Peace

God gave us nature to enjoy, not to be worshipped. My greatest joy comes from serving and helping others, raising my kids, loving my wife, guiding people in discovering God, and enjoying nature and new adventures. If you find yourself unhappy in life, it may be because you are not pursuing your true purpose, which brings fulfillment from within. God commands us to love Him, keep His commandments, and love our neighbors as ourselves. Living according to these simple truths means finding peace no matter your circumstances.

When you actively seek God's will for your life, you will gain peace where you are in life. This doesn't mean your circumstances are permanent; the direction of your life can change. Abraham didn't set down tent pegs when he left his hometown; he kept moving as he followed God's purpose. Living in accordance with God's purpose may not always place you exactly where you want to be, but it will bring you inner peace.

As I strive to fulfill what God has called me to do—loving my wife, teaching my kids, helping others, and sharing the Word of God—I experience great peace. This peace is incredibly profound when I continuously seek God's will for my life, remaining willing to go where He sends me and to do what He instructs. The closer you draw to God with a heart ready to take action, the more you will see Him move in your life.

I have noticed that some of the most depressed individuals are those not aligned with God's will or purpose for their lives. I've also observed those who aren't actively serving others often struggle as well. Proverbs 18:1 says, " He that separates himself seeks *his own* desire, And rages against all sound wisdom." God created moments for solitude, exemplified by Jesus, who often withdrew from the crowds to pray. However, some people choose to isolate themselves and stop serving others or God, which can lead to despair.

Be cautious not to fall into despair, lack hope, or harbor unforgiveness or bitterness during vulnerable moments. A healthy balance between social interaction and solitude is essential as you spend time with God and fulfill His will. Every human alive must learn patience without becoming complacent in prayer and doing good. Everyone must cultivate gratitude and be content with their current circumstances and what they possess in life. 1 Thessalonians 5:16-18: "Rejoice always; pray without ceasing; in everything give thanks: for this is God's will for you in Christ Jesus."

Part of loving God and your neighbor and practicing patience is outlined in 1 Corinthians 13:4-5. "Love suffers long, *and* is kind; love envy not; love is not puffed up, does not behave itself unseemly, seeks not its own, is not provoked, takes no account of evil;" I have found that enjoying life, family, and God while helping others is both rewarding and joyful. If any of these aspects are out of balance, my life also feels out of balance. James 4:7, "Be subject therefore unto God; but resist the devil, and he will flee from you."

    I read some of these verses and believe they are vital for all of us. Philippians 2:12 "So then, my beloved, even as you have always obeyed, not as in my presence only, but now much more in my absence, work out your own salvation with fear and trembling;" John 5:14 "Afterward Jesus finds him in the temple, and said unto him, Behold, you are made whole: sin no more, lest a worse thing happens to you." As we see again in 2 Peter 2:20-21 "For if, after they have escaped the defilements of the world through the knowledge of the Lord and Saviour Jesus Christ, they are again entangled in it and overcome, the last state has become worse with them than the first. For it was better for them not to have known the way of righteousness, than, after knowing it, to turn back from the holy commandment that delivered them."

    How much more should we live out and cherish the grace of God while being careful not to give in to temptation so we can remain at peace? I can attest that every person who has returned to their old way of life appears to be drowning and struggling to stay afloat. Hebrews 3:15 "Today if you shall hear his voice, Harden not your hearts, as in the provocation." 1 John 5:4-5 "For whatsoever is begotten of God overcomes the world: and this is the victory that has overcome the world, *even* our faith. And who is he that overcomes the world, but he that believes that Jesus is the Son of God?" Our most significant purpose is to continue growing in faith through God's grace, which empowers us.
2 Timothy 1:7 says, "For God gave us not a spirit of fearfulness; but of power and love and discipline." We should strive to maintain a sound mind and a life of peace. Like a tree that withstands weather, testing, and trials, we must remain fruitful regardless of the season. Like in 2 Timothy

4:2, which says, "preach the word; be urgent in season, out of season; reprove, rebuke, exhort, with all longsuffering and teaching."

Ephesians 2:8-9 says, "for by grace have you been saved through faith; and that not of yourselves, *it is* the gift of God; not of works, that no man should glory." God's work in all of us is accomplished by His grace and spirit, which is instilled in us through His word. It's up to us to allow this word into our hearts and continue to live by it.

Matthew 28:19-20 says, "Go therefore, and make disciples of all the nations, baptizing them into the name of the Father and of the Son and of the Holy Spirit: teaching them to observe all things whatsoever I commanded you: and know, I am with you always, even unto the end of the world." Knowing God will always be with us is a great joy and comfort. We fulfill our calling on this Earth by walking in His will and purpose. No matter where we go, he will always be with us, speaking to us and guiding us. The more you live by faith, the more He will speak to you. If you draw close to Him, He will draw close to you.

1 Thessalonians 4:3-6. "For this is the will of God, *even* your sanctification, that you abstain from fornication; that each one of you know how to possess himself of his own vessel in sanctification and honor, not in the passion of lust, even as the Gentiles who know not God; that no man transgress, and wrong his brother in the matter: because the Lord is an avenger in all these things, as also we forewarned you and testified."

Loving God and loving your neighbor is God's will for us all. If we continue to live in this way, it will go well for us no matter what happens in our lives. I have experienced many obstacles in my journey with God, but I have found peace through them all as long as I drew near Him. I now understand Romans 8:38-39 "For I am persuaded, that neither death, nor life, nor angels, nor principalities, nor things present, nor things to come, nor powers, nor height, nor depth, nor any other creature, shall be able to separate us from the love of God, which is in Christ Jesus our Lord." What could possibly take you away from God's love once you have experienced it? Can anything in this world rob you of His or your love for him? God's love brings incredible peace.

I recall a flight where a woman's voice over the intercom carried a tone of dread as she instructed everyone to remain seated. I noticed the flight attendants in a panic, rushing up and down the aisle, and I realized something was wrong. I heard God tell me it was a matter of a woman's health, and shortly after, I overheard a flight attendant mention, "She's having trouble breathing; her blood pressure and oxygen levels are very low." Moments later, an announcement was made: "Is there any medical staff onboard?" I hesitated for a moment until I felt God urge me to go. After some time, He prompted me again, saying, "Go pray over her." I approached the back of the plane and explained, "I'm not a doctor, but I'm a pastor who just returned from a mission trip. May I pray with her and for all of you? "The woman I observed, filled with anxiety and incredible stress, took a deep breath and sighed in relief, saying, "Oh my gosh, yes! That is amazing of you; thank you so much!" I knelt beside her with her two small children nearby, who were on a flight for the first time from Venezuela, and I prayed. Within moments, her condition improved. I reassured the flight crew, saying, "She will be okay."

When there is no one to help and nowhere to turn or land, like that plane, who will be there to answer the call? Who will find peace when others are not? Where does that peace come from? Through the many experiences in life where fear ruled the atmosphere, God gave me peace and the ability to take action when others could not. Like I once told many in prison, the story of Daniel, who interpreted the writing on the wall when no one else could. Kings, new agers, witches, fortune tellers, and spiritual seekers—including people from the region—were left without answers. But Daniel, a man who loved God, prayed and lived according to His ways. He did not worship other gods or adopt the practices of those around him. Though he was a busy businessman, he ultimately knew God's eternal purpose for his life. He could read the writing on the wall and explain its meaning to everyone. Shouldn't you strive to be that person for yourself and those around you?

Remember, God's purpose for your life will always be peace—not always outwardly, but within your inner being through the Spirit that gives life. Wherever God leads, go, and don't look back! Do it with joy and peace, and remain set apart! Everyone has the same 24 hours in a day and access to the same Bible. You can choose life and discover purpose when you seek Yeshua (Jesus the Messiah) with all of your heart, soul, and mind. May God bless each one of you! No matter what you go through, keep looking beyond the horizon as the sun rises and sets. Keep sailing along and go where your purpose leads!

I can confidently find peace anywhere in the world because God has helped me discover my life's purpose. Psalm 23:2. "He makes me to lie down in green pastures; He leads me beside still waters." Your sought purpose is to reach the world that is lost. The words of Ecclesiastes 7:16 speak loudly throughout my life. "Be not righteous overmuch; neither make yourself overwise: why should you destroy yourself?" This serves as a reminder always to remain humble and contrite. Don't believe you are holy or religious, nor let the knowledge you've gained puff up your brain like a balloon. Before you take any step in life, ensure that your greatest desire is love for God and your neighbor with deep compassion. God says the humble will be exalted. However, be mindful. God says we are not to dominate any position or control others. Our purpose should be to live by example in our daily lives. Your goal should be to echo the words of 2 Timothy 4:7 before you pass, whether it be early or at an old age. "Be not righteous overmuch; neither make yourself overwise: why should you destroy yourself?"

Before his death, Moses said to God, "If you are pleased with me, teach me your ways so I may know you and continue to find favor with you." He longed to see the land that God had promised him. Are you envisioning the promised land for yourself with a heart like his? God replied to Moses, saying, "My Presence will go with you, and I will give you rest." Moses desired nothing more than God's presence. He had nothing to prove, gain, or need except for the closeness with God and peace with a vision of God's eternal promise. What is the purpose of life?

Solomon says, "Of making many books there is no end, and much study wearies the body." He also says, "Fear God and keep his commandments, for this is the duty of all mankind." But I would like to add something to his wisdom.

      Learn to slow down, enjoy the simple moments, care for others, and enjoy adventuring and laughing much. Never lose sight of God, nor leave his presence and become distracted. Be like water in the world, the lakes, rivers, streams, oceans, ponds, rain, the water you drink, plants it grows, and showers you bathe in. Everyone needs, desires, and finds peace in it and by it. Be the living water that brings life to the world and people. Likewise, everyone loves to be more proactive and happier in the warm sun, be the light like the sun. Bring warmth, happiness, and peace like laying beside the warm ocean waves with the breeze blowing. Be the light and springs of life from God to the world so that they may also discover purpose. Psalm 4:8: "In peace I will lie down and sleep, for you alone, Lord, make me dwell in safety."

      Now go and discover purpose in life, and live out your life of adventure as you prepare for the future that's coming as you continue to strive and live for God's kingdom now on Earth! Shalom!

"Five minutes inside eternity, and we will wish that we had sacrificed more, wept more, grieved more, loved and prayed more, and given more."

-Leonard Ravenhill

The Unanswered Wonders of the Universe, by Todd Aaron

Much has been hidden from our clear view and buried so that we do not see the whole picture and what's hiding behind this earth's horizon and past what we can see. This book helps you discover yourself more in-depth and see the world differently from a whole new perspective. Not only does it help dive deep into the created universe, but it also explores the depths within ourselves. Spiritually, it will draw you closer to God on your journey and help you see the Bible and life in a way that is rarely spoken or discovered.

Available where books are sold!

Made in the USA
Middletown, DE
15 March 2025